PADDLE ROUTES OF WESTERN WASHINGTON

50 Flatwater Trips for Kayak and Canoe

PADDLE ROUTES OF WESTERN WASHINGTON

50 Flatwater Trips for Kayak and Canoe

by
Verne Huser

THE MOUNTAINEERS • SEATTLE

Dedicated to George and Nancy Saling, true friends whose support, assistance and companionship have been invaluable in the creation of this book.

17983

The Mountaineers: Organized 1906 ". . . to explore, study, preserve, and enjoy the natural beauty of the Northwest."

© 1990 by Verne Huser
7 6 5 4 3
5 4 3 2

Published by The Mountaineers
1011 S.W. Klickitat Way, Suite 107, Seattle, Washington 98134
Published simultaneously in Canada by Douglas & McIntyre, Ltd., 1615 Venables Street, Vancouver, B.C. V5L 2H1

Manufactured in the United States of America
Edited by Teresa Danielsen
Cover design and layout by Sally Ketcham
Maps by Amelia M. Budge
Cover photograph by David Harrison
Frontispiece: Lower Green River
Photographs by Verne Huser

Library of Congress Cataloging in Publication Data
Huser, Verne.
  Paddle routes of western Washington : 50 flatwater trips for kayak and canoe / by Verne Huser.
    p. cm.
  Includes bibliographical references.
  ISBN 0-89886-231-0
  1. Canoes and canoeing—Washington (State)—Guide-books.
2. Kayaking—Washington (State)—Guide-books. 3. Washington (State)—Description and travel—1981—Guide-books. I. Title.
GV776.W2H87   1990
797.1'22'09797—dc20   89-49132
                                                            CIP

CONTENTS

REFERENCE MAP

N

BRITISH COLUMBIA

1
2
3
4

8 9
5
11
10 12
13

15 16 17
14
18
22
19
Seattle
25   23 20
21
26
24
27 28

Tacoma
29

43
44
42
41
40

39

35
31
32 34
33
30   36
37 38

Olympia

45

48 49
47
50

PACIFIC

OCEAN

46
COLUMBIA   RIVER

OREGON

Miles
0 10 20 30 40

Washington

Low water levels of late summer narrow rivers, leaving broad beaches for camping.

PREFACE

Twelve years ago when I first began canoeing the rivers of western Washington, I found precious little information about them: where to launch or take out a craft, what class water certain river segments exhibited, what I might expect to experience on the river. This information wasn't readily available.

There were only Werner Furrer's two books (now combined into one—*Water Trails of Washington,* 1979) and Milt Keizer's *Western Steelhead Fishing Guides,* a series of map books for fishermen now available in a single volume. There were paddle clubs whose members ran trips on a number of river segments and who knew the river segments well. I could join a club, which I did, and pick the brains of those who knew the rivers, which I did, but nowhere was there a comprehensive guide to the rivers I wanted to paddle as a beginning canoeist.

Over the years a series of river guides began to appear, for the most part dealing with whitewater. Sea kayaking became extremely popular, and several books appeared for the saltwater paddler. The Mountaineers published Phil Jones's *Canoe Routes: Northwest Oregon* (1982) that included 50 river segments, most of them in the beaver state but a few in Washington. The time was ripe for this book, which has now been 8 years in preparation.

This book, then, is an attempt to provide paddlers with useful information that will enable them to enjoy the rivers and associated waterways of western Washington in crafts powered by human muscle rather than motor—primarily canoes and kayaks. I have scouted all of these river segments, some of them by poling, often **up** the river with the tide, then back down to avoid a shuttle.

Western Washington, with its heavy rainfall and numerous rivers that drain the well-watered land, is an ideal area for canoeing. The rivers were highways in the early days, means of transportation and commerce. Some of them still are, but most of them have become recreational resources today.

While many of these rivers have been altered by human activity (dams, dikes, clear-cuts, population, pollution), some of them are still pristine, certainly valuable get-aways from the noise and stress of modern civilization. It never ceases to amaze me how quickly I can leave behind the contemporary world when I launch my canoe onto the soothing waters of a river:

■ From downtown Redmond I paddle the Sammamish at rush hour along the Sammamish River Parkway, seeing birds and beaver as I drift placidly north, watching a mallard hen with her brood of ducklings, hearing the red-winged blackbird singing in the late afternoon;

■ From Lake Sammamish, where powerboats buzz like angry hornets, I pole up Issaquah Creek, picking blackberries from the bushes that lean over the stream and watching salmon swimming upstream, warblers flitting about, kingfishers and green herons—all within half a mile of I-90;

■ From a roadside fishing access south of Little Rock near Olympia, I launch into what looks like a southern swamp stream, soon losing the sound of logging trucks along Highway 121 on a black-water river fringed by vegetation that mutes the sounds of civilization and masks the fumes with the fragrance of wildflowers.

My purpose in writing this book is to enable people to enjoy the rivers of western Washington safely and with a minimum of impact on these waters and their adjacent shorelines, on the fauna and flora that inhabit these areas, and on other people who use them.

Washington is blessed with many waterways, some of them already badly abused, others rarely used. We can learn to care more about them if we get to know them better, and that's what this book is all about: getting to know western Washington's canoe routes and taking better care of them so that those who come after us—tomorrow or in the next century—may know them as we have and draw both pleasure and spiritual power from them.

ACKNOWLEDGMENTS

I thank the following people for their advice, insight, information and counsel in preparing this book: Paul Agrimes, Dennis Canty, Terry Danielsen, Murray Davis, Tim Davis, Roger De Spain, Al Falco, Wes Felty, Jim Greenleaf, Bob Greenwalt, David Harrison, Willa Huser, Heidi Huser, Gary Korb, Zella Mathews, John and Ratha Miles, James Moore, Lee and Judy Moyer, Ray and Martha Parker, Robert Michael Pyle, Bill Rafferty, George and Nancy Saling, Frank Schultz, Steve Starland, Michael Thomas, Ty Tice, and John Vraspir.

INTRODUCTION

Canoeing has come of age in western Washington. As the Native American canoe has become less common to the point of disappearing, the modern canoe has become ever more popular. The first people to thrive in this area used the canoe as a means of making their living, just as the Indians of the Great Plains used the horse. Few people today use canoes or horses in their livelihood: both have become primarily recreational in their application.

Western Washington was for centuries dominated by canoe routes. Aboriginal inhabitants poled or paddled the rivers and the protected saltwater routes as a way of life. Some of them ventured into the open Pacific to hunt the whale. It is likely that the Yankee clipper ship was patterned after the whaling canoes of Northwest Indians (see Philip Drucker's *Indians of the Northwest Coast*). Even as European, then Asian civilizations made contact with the Indians of the Northwest Coast, they used the canoe routes of the people, adopting their crafts and techniques as well.

As I began researching the rivers of western Washington to include them in this book, it became evident that it was necessary to know how to go upstream as well as down—as the Native Americans had. It was necessary to learn to pole a canoe, to track or line the craft (tow the craft from shore) or simply walk it through the shallows, and thus do without a shuttle.

These techniques are learned by reading, talking with experts, and then practicing—as often as possible with the experts themselves. The techniques are learned by getting out on the rivers and exploring. Exploring is still possible on the rivers of western Washington, and this book is intended to provide the paddler with useful information that will make that exploration easier, safer and more meaningful.

TRIP DESCRIPTIONS

The rivers are listed in logical order from their mouths upstream and from north to south, clockwise around Puget Sound, then up the coast of the Olympic Peninsula, and finally down the coast from Grays Harbor, following the Columbia River upstream from its mouth. The following information is capsulized for each of the 50 trips described in this book in a standardized format for easy reference.

Location. A general location by nearby town or well-known feature is given to locate each river segment.

Distance. The distance in miles is taken from the Washington Department of Fisheries' Catalog of Washington Streams, which indicates the mile-by-mile length of rivers, counting upstream from the mouth. On lakes and saltwater bodies and on the Columbia River tributaries for which the state fishery maps are not available, the mileage is estimated from USGS maps and NOAA charts. Distances will vary depending on the actual route taken by paddlers using the book.

River Time. The guesstimate of time is based on actual on-water measurements, but they are rough approximations because the segments were run at varying water levels, some of the routes were poled (generally faster than paddling), and there were occasional brief stops to take pictures, make notes, watch wildlife, explore landmarks and record times. Numerous factors will influence paddlers' speed (time) relative to that given in this book: type of craft, size of party, level of flow, mishaps. With practice, paddlers will soon be able to judge the relative time it takes them to run a specific river compared to the times given here.

Maps/Charts. U.S. Geological Survey (USGS) maps and National Oceanographic and Atmospheric Administration (NOAA) charts (where available) are given for each trip. The USGS maps are 7.5-minute (7.5′) series or 15-minute (15′) series for the river segment, which may require several maps for some stretches. The NOAA charts are for the coastal areas only but may cover some river mouths (the Skagit, for example) or even whole rivers (the Sammamish, for example).

Best Season. Most rivers in this book can be run year-round. A few of them, however, may be too low in late summer or early fall. During heavy rains or spring runoff, many of them may be too high to run safely. As a general rule, if the water level is up in the shrubbery, paddlers should think seriously before launching a trip. If too many gravel bars or mud flats are showing, the river may be too low. Water levels fluctuate seasonally and, on reservoir-release rivers and in tidal areas, daily. Flow information on many of the popular rivers is available by calling the NOAA hotline (526-8530). A local paddle club may also have this information.

Hazards. While the river segments covered in this book are relatively mild (Class II at the most difficult), there are certain hazards: **sweepers,** trees overhanging the river bank that can sweep paddlers out of their crafts; **obstacles** such as rocks, logjams and trees in or completely across the river; **cold water,** which can lead to hypothermia (loss of body heat); **contrary tides** that run counter to the direction of intent; **wind, fog** and other weather conditions that can make canoeing dangerous. Specific potential hazards are listed for each segment.

Shuttle. A brief description of the shuttle is given for each river segment, including the distance, the road condition, and suggested vehicle where appropriate (bicycle, mountain bike, 4-wheel-drive vehicle, standard vehicle).

Rating. The International Scale of River Difficulty includes six classes from easy to difficult. Class I designates moving water with a few riffles and small waves and few or no obstructions. Class II involves easy rapids with waves up to 3 feet, and wide, clear channels that are obvious without scouting (studying the rapid before entering it), but some maneuvering is required.

Classes III to VI are increasingly difficult, but since none of the river segments in this book are in that range of difficulty, they are not described here. A designation of Class I– or I would indicate a very easy section of river with little current, no waves and no obstacles. A Class I+ would suggest a section of river approaching Class II, above the difficulty of Class I but not yet Class II.

In this book, each trip is rated by the following system:

A Equivalent to Class I– or I. Still water or rivers with current less than 2 mph, benign rivers suitable for novices;

B Equivalent to Class I+ or II–. River segments with current between 2 and 4 mph, some maneuvering skills required;

C Equivalent to Class II or II+. River segments with a velocity of more than 4 mph or with rapids, sharp turns, or obstacles that require significant maneuvering;

T Tidal with varying class ratings, indicated by A, B, or C, that involve paddling tidal waters, whether that be saltwater stretches of bays and harbors or tidal reaches of rivers.

Some segments may be given two ratings indicating that they are tidal but also have other characteristics worth noting. The signs + and – are used to indicate a slightly more difficult rating (B+, for example, means more difficult than a B but not as difficult as a C) or a slightly easier rating (B– means less difficult than a B but not as easy as an A).

Paddling, even on quiet streams with slow currents and few obstacles, entails unavoidable risks that every paddler assumes, understands, and agrees to take on. The fact that a section of river is described in this book and is rated for difficulty does not mean that it necessarily will be safe for a particular paddler or at a particular water level. Because rivers are dynamic systems, conditions vary from year to year, season to season, even day to day. Accordingly, so does the amount of preparation and knowledge required to enjoy them safely. If in doubt about their own qualifications, prospective paddlers will find many books and courses that offer the information and training needed to take these trips safely. This book offers some tips, but it is not intended to substitute for good instruction from an experienced river paddler.

These warnings are not intended to frighten qualified paddlers from taking the river trips described herein. The great majority of paddlers enjoy safe trips down these rivers every year with adequate knowledge and preparation. But paddlers should exercise their own independent judgment and common sense.

A NOTE ABOUT SAFETY

Safety is an important concern in all outdoor activities. No guidebook can alert you to every hazard or anticipate the limitations of every reader. Therefore, the descriptions of roads, trails, rivers, routes, and natural features in this book are not representations that a particular place or excursion will be safe for your party. When you follow any of the river routes described in this book, you assume responsibility for your own safety. Under normal conditions, such excursions require the usual attention to traffic, road and trail conditions, weather, water, terrain, the capabilities of your party, and other factors. Keeping informed on current conditions and exercising common sense are the keys to a safe, enjoyable outing.

CHOICE OF CRAFT

Flatwater boaters have several choices in crafts, but most will use canoes or kayaks. Other possibilities include inflatable crafts, either small rafts or canoes/kayaks; dories or driftboats, flat-bottomed row-boats with flared sides and heavy rocker (bow-to-stern curvature); and Sportyaks, small hard-hulled dinghies.

River runners on Class I and II waters have two levels of choice: (1) whether to row or to paddle and (2) which specific craft to use for rowing or paddling.

Rowing Crafts

Rowing crafts include rafts, dories and Sportyaks. They are generally operated with oars mounted on the craft or attached to a frame that is fixed to the craft.

Rafts. As discussed in this book, rafts are inflatable crafts, varying in design from inexpensive one- and two-person single-chamber toys made of vinyl to professional crafts with several air chambers and a cloth fabric coated with a rubberized material. The cheap rafts without a fabric base will not stand the wear and tear of river use nor will they respond to control by oar or paddle; they should not be considered for any kind of river trip above an A rating in this book. They are usually too insubstantial to be inflated to adequate air pressure and do not

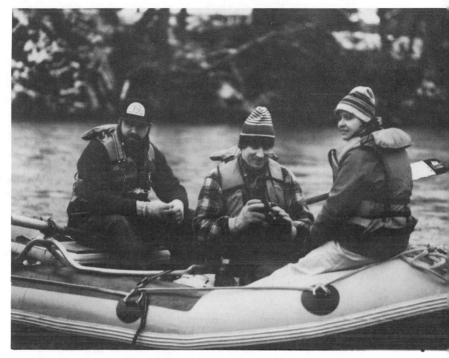

Rafters drift the Skagit River through Marblemount.

respond well to rowing. They are sometimes paddled (see below under Paddle Crafts).

Most of the smaller rafts are equipped with oarlocks of some kind, but many of them are unreliable. If rafts do not come with oarlocks—or if they do, but the oarlocks are inadequate—it may pay to build or buy a frame that can be fixed to the raft. Heavy-duty oarlocks made of wood or metal can then be mounted on the frame, giving the rower a better position for powering the craft and controlling its movements.

Dories. These hard-hulled, specialized rowboats have been developed for river use. They have heavy rocker—exaggerated bow-to-stern (front-to-back) convexity—flared sides, and a sharp prow (forward part of the boat's hull). They are popular among fishermen, who often equip them with a motor. Since this book deals in muscle-powered crafts, it will not discuss the use of motors. The dory is powered and maneuvered with a single set of oars.

Sportyaks. These dinghies are small, highly specialized plastic rowboats (some people call them plastic bathtubs) designed as one-person

15

fishing boats. They fit nicely into the back of a pickup truck, and they are lightweight and maneuverable, extremely riverworthy, and fun to row with a single pair of 5- or 6-foot oars. However, they do not move through the water with any speed and are not recommended for slow-water or saltwater trips. Sportyaks come with built-in oarlocks, but you can improve reliability by adding a metal frame to which a heavy-duty oarlock and even a suspended seat are attached.

Paddle Crafts

Paddle crafts include canoes, kayaks and inflatable boats of two basic kinds: rafts and inflatable canoe/kayaks. They are powered and maneuvered by paddles, either single- or double-bladed.

In the world of modern boating, there are two basic differences between canoes and kayaks, since both may be decked and look similar: (1) canoes are paddled with a single-bladed paddle and kayaks, with a double-bladed paddle; (2) canoes are paddled from a kneeling position (or from a seat suspended well above water level) and kayaks are paddled from a sitting position on a low seat at or near water level. These may seem subtle distinctions, but they are important differences.

Canoes. Canoes are long, narrow, hard-hulled crafts patterned after American Indian designs. Aesthetic and practical, canoes come in numerous forms, sizes, colors, and materials, from traditional wood-and-canvas to space-age fabrics. Some canoes are better for still-water use on lakes; others, for moving water in rivers.

Most people think of canoes as open crafts, but many modern canoes are decked to enable them to operate more effectively in heavy white-water. People do run Class III and IV, even Class V rapids in canoes.

River canoes should have little or no keel (a raised ridge that runs the length of the underside of the craft and tends to make the canoe track, or move in a straight line), have sides high enough to keep out the waves that might be encountered in mild rapids, and be sturdy enough to withstand some contact with obstacles (logs, rocks, the river bank and bottom).

Canoes are made of wood and canvas (traditional), aluminum, fiberglass and a whole family of artificial materials commonly known as plastics. A few people still make and use bark canoes, but such crafts are rare. Many wood-and-canvas canoes still exist, but relatively few are produced today. Purely wooden canoes, such as cedar strippers, are things of great beauty, but the hand-crafting that goes into them makes them too expensive or too personal for everyday use; they are sturdy but require regular maintenance.

Most modern paddlers use aluminum, fiberglass, or plastic canoes. Aluminum is noisy, it conducts heat (and therefore cold), and while it holds its shape in normal use, it can be badly damaged in a traumatic situation. Fiberglass canoes are about as heavy as aluminum ones but are easier to repair; however, they do not hold their form well nor do they take the shock of serious collision as well as the modern plastics.

The plastic revolution of the past few decades has altered the canoeing industry more than any other single innovation. More plastic canoes are sold each year than were in operation a decade ago.While some of the space-age fabrics are extremely expensive, mass production has brought the price down, and many of the fabrics offer fantastic strength, lightness and durability.

There is no perfect canoe that will do all things for all users. Probably the best overall material for canoes today is the foam-and-plastic sandwich used by several manufacturers under various trade names. In the field research for this book an 18-foot aluminum canoe, a 16-foot plastic canoe and a 12-foot foam-and-plastic sandwich canoe each gave good service in different ways.

A good lake canoe is not a good river canoe. The longer the canoe, in general, the faster it will move, but the more difficult it is to turn. On a river, paddlers will want to be able to turn the canoe quickly to avoid obstacles. Before buying a canoe, go on a few trips in a rented or borrowed canoe. Go with a local paddle club, both for safety and to experience the variety of paddle crafts available.

Talk to dealers. Read the literature (manufacturers' brochures, how-to books, accounts in paddling magazines). Talk to other paddlers; hang out in the paddle shops. Paddlers should take their time in choosing a canoe.

Decked canoes look a lot like kayaks and can be used very much as kayaks are used. None of the river segments in this book require the protection of a decked canoe, but there is certainly no reason a decked canoe couldn't be used.

Kayaks. A creation of the Eskimo culture, kayaks might be considered more garment than boat: paddlers wear them rather than sit in them. Eskimos, who used them to hunt seals, walrus and whales in the frigid ocean, learned to roll them as a life-saving technique. If the crafts tipped over in the waves, the kayakers simply rolled back to an upright position and never really got wet because the craft was worn, each paddler enclosed in a waterproof garment married to the craft. Used in Europe in various modifications for decades, they have also become popular as recreational crafts in North America. Kayaks are now common on Northwestern rivers.

Many early kayaks were made of wood and canvas, but a few were all wood and even fewer, aluminum. Fiberglass swept the market shortly after World War II as hundreds of paddlers began making their own crafts. It remains a popular low-cost fabric for kayaks, but most river paddlers have followed the plastic revolution.

A second revolution has been the development of flatwater touring

Kayakers on the Sauk River.

kayaks, especially for sea kayaking. Usually fitted with a rudder (often controlled by the feet), such kayaks are easier to paddle than canoes, even for beginners. However, they may be difficult to handle on sharp turns and in the relatively mild whitewater of Class II rapids.

Kayaks are decked crafts, less roomy than canoes for gear and people. However, they come in one- and two-person models, with a few larger ones capable of carrying three people. Since this book generally deals with short segments that can normally be paddled in a day, there is little need to carry much gear along unless an overnight trip is planned. And even overnighters can often be done by car camping. The paddlers leapfrog down the river, canoeing or kayaking to the shuttle vehicle, where the camp gear is kept.

Folding kayaks, which have been in use for half a century or more, offer an interesting alternative. They are lightweight and fold into small packages for easy storage and transport. Most of them have sturdy frames and a rubberized fabric hull. Inflatable kayaks have improved over the past two decades and offer another alternative, especially if storage space is critical (see discussion below).

Inflatables. The inflatable crafts include both rafts and inflatable canoes/kayaks (some manufacturers call them canoes, others call them kayaks, but in fact they are neither).

Paddle rafts are simply inflatable rafts that are powered and controlled by paddlers. One, two or more paddlers, depending on the size of the craft, sit or kneel on the floor, or more frequently, sit on the side tubes of larger rafts and try to make the craft go where a common goal suggests it should.

Some paddle rafts are specially designed with a series of thwarts (cross tubes) for greater stability and to give paddlers something to brace against to help them stay in the raft. However, they are expensive. Occasionally rafts used primarily for paddle-powered trips are equipped with toe-hold straps fastened to the floor for better bracing. (**Danger:** never use foot loops big enough to allow a foot to become entrapped; in case of a capsize, the paddler could be trapped in a life-threatening situation.)

Inflatable canoes/kayaks are elongated inflatable crafts that are neither canoe nor kayak since they are not decked like a kayak but are normally paddled like a kayak. They cannot be Eskimo-rolled as a kayak can, and the paddler simply sits on the bottom of the craft, not in a seat set into the floor. Such crafts generally do not track as well as hard-hulled boats, but they are forgiving and adaptable and can be stored and transported with minimal space and hassle. They are subject to puncture, of course, but many modern fabrics are reasonably sturdy if they involve a cloth base permeated with a rubberized material.

Craft Selection

Any of the crafts mentioned above can be used on the rivers discussed in this book, but certain crafts will work better in specific situations. Weigh the options. What is needed, a small craft with little carrying capacity that one paddler can operate or a boat that will take the whole family along? Do the paddlers want to run Class II rapids or dink around the saltwater sloughs? Do the paddlers want a fast craft that can take the rapids but requires expertise to maneuver or a more stable craft that any fool can manage?

Rafts, especially the larger ones, have the greatest carrying capacity, and they are stable and forgiving. Open canoes, especially the longer ones, can carry a lot of gear and people, but they are less forgiving than a raft. The Sportyak, a one-person craft, has little carrying capacity, but one person can handle it nicely—it weighs only 38 pounds and is riverworthy enough to negotiate the worst rapids mentioned in this book.

Sportyaks and rafts, however, whether they are paddled or rowed, do not make much headway on flatwater. Paddle rafts will be better than Sportyaks for such passive waters, but canoes will be better than either because they cut through the water more efficiently. Sea kayaks may be the best bet, but the carrying capacity of kayaks is somewhat limited, and they require real skill to manage and maneuver.

Dories are remarkably maneuverable and have fantastic carrying capacity, but they are so heavy and bulky they require a trailer for transport to and from the river. Inflatables require pumps to inflate and the time to inflate them—paddlers can't just throw them in the water and be off. Rowing rafts require rigging (marrying the frame to the craft) in addition to the time and effort it takes to inflate them.

Paddlers need to know what their needs are and how best to satisfy them within the characteristics of the crafts available for negotiating these relatively quiet waters: carrying capacity, lightness of weight, quickness of launch, ease of transport, hull design, stability, maneuverability, level of skill required to manage the craft, durability, and maintenance.

EQUIPMENT

Good equipment increases the enjoyment of the river experience and adds to safety. It pays to have good equipment and to keep it in good repair.

Craft-related

In addition to the craft itself, you need to consider other craft-related equipment: paddles, poles, and other devices for propelling and controlling the craft, and transportation for getting the craft to and from the river.

Propulsion and Control. Equipment for propelling and controlling a craft includes paddles for canoes, kayaks and paddle rafts; poles for poling canoes; oars and oarlocks for dories, Sportyaks and rowing rafts; and frames for rafts, perhaps even for Sportyaks.

Canoe paddles, which are also used on paddle rafts, come in different lengths, widths, and shapes. There are even bent-shaft paddles used by marathon and downriver canoe racers and by a growing number of recreational paddlers because they are more efficient.

The grip of a paddle, its length, the width of the blade, the contour of the shaft are very personal considerations, but you will want a paddle that floats, that is strong enough to do its job, yet light enough not to tire the paddler, durable, balanced, and aesthetically pleasing. A general rule for canoe-paddle length used to be "from nose to toes," but the current trend is for shorter paddles, perhaps from toe to chin. For bent-shaft paddles, it is crotch to chin for length of shaft, from the grip to the bend.

In general, stern paddles should be slightly longer than bow paddles (especially if the bow paddler is shorter than the stern paddler). For paddle rafting, paddles should be several inches longer than for canoeing because the paddler, sitting on the tube, is farther from the water.

Paddlers who use a short, choppy stroke, such as Native American paddlers or marathon and downriver racers will want a shorter, narrower paddle than those who like to use a long, slow stroke.

Kayak paddles are longer than canoe paddles and have a blade at each end, usually at right angles to each other. The double-bladed paddle enables the kayaker to keep a steady side-to-side rhythm during normal paddling. Kayak paddle blades are often curved or cupped, the concave surface serving as the power face (the side that exerts pressure against the water). For flatwater paddling, a slightly longer paddle is needed than for whitewater paddling, perhaps as long as 8 feet; the more whitewater encountered, the shorter the paddle should be. Paddle length is also related to the height or the arm-length of the paddler.

Wooden paddles are traditional and beautiful, especially laminated ones, but they do not wear as well as plastic or fiberglass ones or those coated with fiberglass. Modern combinations of metal and plastic or just plastic are durable but garish, coming in many different colors and color combinations. It is up to the paddlers, but they should look over the assortment at the local paddle shop and explore the options by collecting information from professional paddlers and other boaters.

For rowing, oarlocks and a pair of oars are needed. These too are available in modern plastics, but many rowers prefer traditional wooden oars. Oars should be roughly 2/3 the length of the craft to be rowed (6-foot oars for a 9-foot boat, 10-foot oars for a 15-foot boat). Many small inflatable rafts and all Sportyaks have built-in oarlocks, but they may not be adequate for serious rowing.

One answer is a rowing frame made of wood or metal, such as those used on virtually all rowing rafts, to which oarlocks are attached. These frames are especially important on larger rafts, but keep in mind that all rafts can be paddled as well as rowed.

Frames made of wood can easily be fashioned at home. They usually rest on top of the inflated tubes and are lashed to the boat with straps attached to D-rings. Sometimes they have floor boards suspended from them to add to the raft's carrying capacity. In any case they will have an oar-mount stand on either side for attaching the oarlocks.

Metal frames made of aluminum or steel pipe tubing generally nest into the center of the raft between the thwarts. They may have suspended floors to increase their carrying capacity (gear dropped into the bottom of an inflatable craft has a tendency to damage the floor when the floor fabric is crimped between gear and river rocks). Many of the professionally built metal frames include a slot for an ice chest or cooler, which then serves as a seat for the rower. Metal frames can also be fitted with oar-mounts for attaching the oarlocks.

Transportation. A means of transporting craft is essential unless the paddlers live on the river bank and make all their trips on one river. Pickup trucks, vans, conventional automobiles using cartop carriers and special boat trailers are used to convey boats to and from the river. Simple and effective cartop carriers can be purchased or created. Metal or tough plastic stiltlike clips that fasten onto the rain gutters of a car can be used. Joining two sets of these with two 2x4s creates a pair of racks for carrying a canoe. Kayaks should be hauled in formfitting cradles. Similar racks made of pipes instead of 2x4s are more expensive but equally effective. Foam padding on the pipe racks saves wear and tear on the craft carried. Be sure to tie the crafts well—front, back and across the top. Nothing can be as disheartening as ruining a good water craft and as disastrous as causing an accident through one careless mistake.

Sportyaks fit nicely into a standard pickup truck bed (or a minitruck long bed) or on a cartop carrier. Many inflatables will easily fit into a standard car trunk, but the larger ones may require a pickup truck bed, a van, or a trailer. Most river runners have their own techniques and methods, their own trailers or racks—go on a few club trips and see their methods.

Dories require a trailer, and inflatable rafts with their frames in place can be hauled to and from the river by flatbed trailer to save time. Canoe- and kayak-carrying trailers can be rented or borrowed for large-party trips.

Personal

Personal gear on a river trip should be kept to a minimum, but always take along anything and everything, you might need. The old 90/10 pattern fits: 90 percent of what paddlers take along will be used only 10 percent of the time; but if they don't have it along, they could be in trouble. Make check lists and use them, add to them and pare them down to the practical, the necessary.

Dry Bags. Waterproof bags are essential for keeping important items dry: maps, sleeping bags, food, cameras—whatever should be kept secure from the water. This is a never-ending problem on river trips and one that has been addressed successfully by a number of manufacturers in recent years.

A wide variety of dry bags, boxes and containers can be used, not all of them the expensive commercial types. A heavy-duty plastic bag within a nylon bag is very satisfactory: the inner bag keeps everything dry, and the outer bag protects the inner bag from tears and punctures. If you spend a lot of time on the river, it may pay to purchase one of the commercial dry bags.

The old stand-by for many river runners is the military surplus ammo can, which comes in several sizes. Be sure the rubber seals are intact.

Clothing. Plan to take along a change of clothes if there is any possibility of getting wet—and there is always that possibility. In winter, wear pile or wool; in summer, protect eyes, head, limbs and torso against the sun. A wet suit or a dry suit may be appropriate on cold-water rivers or during cold weather; and in the Pacific Northwest, good rain gear is essential.

Even if wearing sandals, shorts and a tank-top on a river trip, always have along a long-sleeved shirt, long pants, dry sox and shoes in case of a wetting. Carry a wool shirt and a wool cap in case of hypothermia, and even a down sleeping bag in winter.

Food and Drink. Ammo cans, ice chests, coolers and thermos bottles, preferably the metal type, can hold food and drink. It may be wise to carry along some extra high-energy food for dealing with hypothermia on winter or cold-water trips. Hot coffee, tea or chocolate is nice to have on those midwinter eagle-watching trips, and cold lemonade is great on a hot summer day. Soggy sandwiches are unpalatable: best keep them dry through proper packing and storing.

Recreational Equipment. Paddlers may include fishing gear, cameras, binoculars, Frisbees, horseshoes, soccer balls, volleyballs and nets among their recreational gear, but the river itself provides many of the accouterments for recreational activities. There are skipping stones, rocks for the Olympic Rock Throw or to throw at floating sticks or bits of bark or hollow trees across the river, and beaches on which to draw pictures or write messages.

Navigational Aids. Maps and charts and compasses are important for planning trips and useful to have along in waterproof cases. Notes from a previous trip or from a friend can be useful, too, to find the take-out or the best campsite. Guidebooks, field guides and area descriptions are all good to have along to provide reference information and enhance the quality of the trip.

Safety

A few rules and regulations are in force on some of the rivers of western Washington relating to carrying personal flotation devices, or PFDs (Coast Guard Regulations), the wearing of PFDs (National Park Service regulations on some rivers within NPS boundaries), the wearing of PFDs and helmets (on the Skykomish east of the Big Eddy; a Snohomish County Ordinance), but Washington remains one of the two states that does not have a state safe-boating law.

The most important safety item is the personal flotation device (PFD), sometimes referred to as a life jacket. First aid kits, repair kits and emergency equipment are also important to have along.

Flotation. Both PFDs and extra flotation for the craft are essential for a safe river trip. The PFD is the single most important item of safety equipment. Be sure it contains adequate flotation, that it is the right size (it may be wise to test it in a swimming pool to be sure), and that it is worn properly. PFDs should be worn at all times on the river, both for the paddlers' safety and for the lesson it suggests to others. PFDs can't save paddlers' lives if they're not worn.

The commonly used horse-collar jackets are not adequate for most adults and are inappropriate for children. Get a good PFD for each member of the family who plans to go on the river. Modern PFDs are comfortable, even stylish, and many come with zipper fronts and pockets for carrying items needed or useful on the river.

Extra flotation in the craft itself is unnecessary in a Sportyak, raft or dory; essential in a kayak; and often appropriate for a canoe. Flotation can be in the form of foam blocks, sheets of ethylfoam, or air bags that can be purchased at any whitewater shop. Even inflated inner tubes will serve: anything that will displace water and help keep the craft afloat when it is full of water—and with the extra flotation in place, the craft won't be so full of water. Extra flotation is a safety factor, a common-sense addition to the margin of safety in any craft used on the paddle routes described in this book.

Anticipation of Emergency Needs. Assuring safety lies largely in anticipation and planning, in providing the means for handling any possibility. Bow- and stern-lines on canoes, grab loops on both ends of kayaks, chicken lines around rafts, throw lines on all crafts, extra rope (well tied to the craft, coiled and secured so it will not create a hazard in the water), and a first aid kit are all important items worth carrying along on every river trip. So is a repair kit with everything needed to at least temporarily repair the craft and its accouterments (such as spare parts for the air pump on an inflatable craft, a spare oarlock for any rowing rig, a craft-specific patch kit, or a spare paddle).

Bailing devices should be carried in every craft, and a sponge can come in handy for sopping up the last bit of water and cleaning up the craft. If too much water is shipped or the craft capsizes, paddlers will have to stop and dump the water or bail the craft thoroughly before continuing the trip.

Emergency Gear. Such gear includes extras of almost everything paddlers might need, from PFDs to a towel and dry clothing, matches and a whistle. Many frequent paddlers wear a whistle on the zipper of their PFD and such emergency items as matches, knife, flashlight and minimal first aid kit tucked away in a waterproof container in the PFD pockets.

POWER AND CONTROL TECHNIQUES

No matter what craft is selected, paddlers need to learn how to power and maneuver it on the river. Initially paddlers should read everything possible about handling the craft that has been chosen. For canoeing it is hard to beat the American National Red Cross book, *Canoeing*. For kayaking, try *Kayaking* by J. Evans and Robert R. Anderson. Cecile Kuhn's *River Rafting* is a good book on rafting (my own *River Running* is out of print, and William McGinnis's *Whitewater Rafting* may be too intimidating for Class I and II boaters). See Further Reading for additional reading and suggestions.

As a general rule keep in mind the fact that for every action there is a counter action. That is, if the water is pushed in one direction with an oar or paddle, the craft will move in the opposite direction. If the handle of an oar is pulled toward the paddler, the water pushed by the oar blade moves away from the paddler (the oarlock serving as a fulcrum), and the boat moves in the direction of the pull.

Water forced against an obstacle piles up against it, then moves around that obstacle at a higher rate of speed to a lower level of the river. The water then slows down and may move back upstream to fill the hole created downstream of that obstacle. The surface of a river is a complex of currents moving in several directions at once. The term *reading the river* refers to learning to determine which way the currents flow by observing its surface and adjusting paddling or rowing strokes to that dynamic medium.

Although the water surface reveals much, subsurface currents also need to be considered. They are reflected on the surface but can be determined to some extent by looking beneath the surface, if the water is clear enough, to study the rocks and logs and other obstacles that give the surface its characteristic appearance. It is understanding the surface appearance that ultimately enables paddlers to read the river and negotiate their way through the conflicting currents. (See my *River Running* for more detail.)

Rowing

Rowing any craft involves using a set of oars mounted on a fulcrum known as an oarlock, which in turn is mounted on the craft to be rowed. The technique is pretty much the same for any craft, though it varies with the size and weight of boat and, to some extent, the nature of the water.

Rafts. Rowing a raft requires a sturdy frame securely attached to the inflatable boat. The oarlocks are mounted on the frame, and the rower sits on the frame and maneuvers the craft by pulling or pushing on the grip end of the oars. The raft is positioned across the current with one oar upstream, the other, downstream to move the craft across the current. The rower essentially selects the current that is going to take the raft where it should go, then rows into that current. Additional maneuvering may be required to avoid an obstacle, to slow the craft, or to make a turn. Positioning the craft at an angle to the current and rowing either diagonally upstream or down to cross the current is called ferrying. The raft can be swiveled by pushing on one oar and pulling on the other, pivoting the craft quickly to reposition it for the next maneuver. The tighter the contact between raft and rowing frame and the higher the air pressure within the raft, the better the craft will respond to its oars.

Dories. Rowing a dory is very similar to rowing a raft, but the dory is more maneuverable. It may be heavier than a raft, depending on its load, but because of the small area in contact with the water relative to its large volume (because of its flared sides and heavy rocker), a dory can turn very quickly. Dories track better than rafts, and they require little water to float them. They are not quite as forgiving as rafts, but that is not usually a factor on Class I and II water.

Sportyaks. Rowing a Sportyak involves short, quick strokes because the oars are shorter and can be moved much more rapidly. They are similar to dories in their maneuverability though they are much lighter, relatively speaking, and float like corks. In waves it is important to keep the bow turned into the crest or the wave may swamp the boat (it will still float even when it is full of water, but why be uncomfortable?) or even flip the lightweight craft.

Paddling

When a craft is paddled, the paddler's lower hand serves as the fulcrum: the power exerted is applied to the water and creates a counter action, whether in a horizontal direction to make the craft move forward, sideways or obliquely, or in a vertical direction to stabilize the craft as in a brace (applying the paddle blade flat to the surface of the water with a vertical pressure, thereby bracing the craft against a capsize).

Canoes. Paddling a canoe is done with a single-bladed paddle from a kneeling position on the bottom of the canoe or from a sitting position, utilizing the seats with which most canoes are equipped. (Whitewater paddlers use straps across their thighs for greater marriage of paddler to craft in the kneeling position for better bracing.)

Northwest Indians do not talk about paddling a canoe so much as they do "pulling" a canoe, a principle—or a way of looking at it—that suggests planting the paddle in the water vertically and pulling the canoe toward that planted paddle. That is essentially what paddlers do when they paddle a canoe: place the paddle in the water—in front, behind, to the side—and pull (or push) the canoe toward (or away from) that point.

Basic strokes for canoeing include the forward stroke (planting the paddle forward of the paddler's position in the canoe and pulling the canoe forward as the paddle moves backward in the water), the back stroke or backpaddle (planting the paddle behind the paddler's position and pulling the canoe backward as the paddle moves forward in the water), the draw stroke (planting the paddle as far to the side as possible and pulling the canoe toward the paddle as the paddle moves toward the canoe), and the pry (planting the paddle next to the gunnel [side] of the canoe and pushing the canoe away from the paddle as the paddle moves away from the canoe).

Variations of these strokes are the J-stroke, which involves a twisting of the paddle into a kind of rudder to correct the canoe's variance from a straight-line route; the sweep stroke, which is a variation of either a forward or a backward stroke and a draw or pry, depending on where the stroke is started and where it ends; and the brace, which is used to maintain the balance of the canoe in rough water or in confusing currents, especially when the canoe is tipping too far to one side or the other, on the verge of capsizing.

But the high brace is more than a defensive stroke. It can be part of an efficient quick-turning stroke in which the paddlers lean far to the side—essentially a draw stroke with a severe lean of the body that ends

A solo canoeist on the South Fork of the Stillaguamish.

in a brace (the reason whitewater paddlers use thigh straps). Eddies are areas of water moving counter to the main current. They occur below (that is, downstream from) obstacles: midstream rocks or logs, promontories or projections from the bank. An eddy is an ideal place for a turn; it helps the paddlers make the maneuver. The bow of the canoe is moved into the eddy with a draw stroke by the bow paddler in a tandem (two-person) canoe (or by the lone paddler of a solo canoe), while the stern paddler and the power of the current on the stern snuggle the canoe into the protective eddy. This is known as an eddy turn, and it is useful for landing, launching, and maneuvering back and forth across the current.

It will take some practice, and it works better if the paddlers have someone to teach them. Read about the techniques in a how-to book, which this isn't. Take a lesson from a proficient paddler or as part of a paddle club's regular activities. The importance of beginning a canoeing career with a paddle club or with friends who know how to handle a canoe cannot be stressed enough.

Remember, too, that the longer a canoe, the faster it moves in a straight line, but the harder it is to turn. Conversely, the shorter it is, the easier it turns, but another factor, rocker, is involved. Rocker is the bow-to-stern convexity of the hull in the water: the greater the rocker, the easier the craft turns.

Tandem canoeing involves two people paddling a canoe together, one in the bow and one in the stern, normally paddling on opposite sides. Solo paddling obviously involves only one person paddling a canoe, usually from somewhere near the center of the craft. Tandem paddlers soon learn to coordinate their strokes for greater efficiency and stability, but here, too, some instruction can be helpful.

All the strokes can be done from a sitting position, but they are all more powerful and effective when done from a kneeling position. Kneeling also tends to lower the center of gravity in a canoe and thereby increase its stability. Many recreational paddlers alternate sitting and kneeling, going to the latter in the rapids, on quick turns, or in any potentially unstabilizing situation—such as trying to avoid a sweeper (overhanging tree).

For long-term paddling a semi-kneeling position with the buttocks resting on the edge of the seat may be more comfortable. Paddlers with arthritic knees may be able to manage by changing position slightly every few minutes. Stretching the bad leg out is helpful also.

Kayaks. Paddling a kayak is done with a double-bladed paddle by one or two persons, depending on the configuration of the craft. Most experienced kayakers use a paddle with blades at roughly right angle to each other; right-handed paddlers will want the left blade up (away from the water's surface) when the right blade is in the water making a power stroke. The reverse is true for left-handed paddlers.

Paddle clubbers, ready to launch, find safety in numbers.

In general, kayak paddle strokes are shallower and at a shallower angle than canoe paddle strokes, primarily because of the double-bladed paddle. But the principle is much the same: move the water in one direction and the kayak will respond in another. Kayak paddle strokes usually alternate from side to side (again, because of the double-bladed paddle), giving the course a slight wiggle unless the wiggle is corrected by a countering rudder stroke.

Kayaks are more maneuverable than canoes, but the same facts hold true: the longer the craft, the harder it is to turn, but the faster it moves in a straight line; the more rocker, the easier the craft turns; the shorter the craft, the easier it turns. Having a rudder, as most sea kayaks do, also makes the craft easier to turn on flatwater. But while the rudder is no substitute for proper paddling technique, it does help turn the longer craft on open water. All this means that for flatwater paddling, a longer kayak is more appropriate; for whitewater paddling, the shorter craft is better.

Since the kayak in general turns more easily than a canoe (because most of them are shorter and have greater rocker), the strokes used to control and power it are more subtle, often a combination of two canoe strokes in one, as in the sweep strokes. The simplest turning pattern is using more power on one side than on the other. The stern rudder is a good solo stroke, but is a more powerful maneuver done by the stern paddler of a tandem kayak: the paddler places one end of the paddle into the water as a rudder, holding the blade against the current to execute a turn toward the side on which the rudder is made.

Braces are vital to the kayaker because a kayak is less forgiving than a canoe. The paddler needs to be more alert to subtle changes in lateral currents, more conscious of the brace as a defensive measure. However, since the kayaker is partially enclosed in the craft and the kayak has a lower center of gravity (because the paddler is sitting so low in the water), there is a compensating stability factor, especially in the touring kayaks that have been developed for flatwater paddling.

Also, the double-bladed paddle offers a compensatory advantage that enables the paddler to react to either side much more quickly than a canoe paddler,who might have to switch sides to execute a brace on the appropriate side.

Most of the strokes used by a canoe paddler with a single-bladed paddle can be used by a kayak paddler (you can't pry or use a J-stroke in a kayak), but because of the nature of kayak paddling—the paddler's position and the double-bladed paddle—most of the strokes are used in a modified manner that will come clear only as they are applied.

As with canoeing, it is important to get some basic instruction in kayak paddling. This is best done with a club group or a commercial instructor. Many whitewater and sea kayaking equipment stores and shops offer such instruction as a means of satisfying their customers' needs and of expanding the sport.

Rafts. Paddling rafts has become a major sport in the Pacific Northwest during the 1980s as dozens of commercial river outfitters have offered paddle raft trips on most of the whitewater rivers of the region. The same crafts and techniques can be applied to the less rambunctious rivers described in this book.

The basic technique involves sitting on the side of the raft (on its inflated tube) and wielding a paddle somewhat longer than a canoe paddle (longer because the paddler is sitting slightly higher above the water than in a canoe).The basic paddle strokes are the same as in canoeing: forward, backward, draw and pry, but they are usually applied through four orders from the captain of a paddle-raft crew:

forward, a command that means simply everyone paddle forward;

backpaddle, a command that means for everyone to paddle backward;

right turn, a command that directs those on the right side to paddle backward and those on the left to paddle forward; and

left turn, a command that directs those on the left side to paddle backward and those on the right to paddle forward.

It may take some practice for the crew to get coordinated. It is important to have a captain in charge so everyone works together. It is also important for the craft to be inflated to a tightness that makes it go where it is directed and for the paddlers to have a means of gripping the raft with their legs, feet, toes so they are not thrown out of the craft by wave action or the raft's striking obstacles.

Smaller rafts may be more of a problem. Because smaller rafts are often made of cheaper material, they can withstand less air pressure and are consequently less rigid and less maneuverable; therefore they are not as likely to track or go where they are intended to go.

Poling

Poling is traditional among Northwestern Indians. As recently as 40 years ago the Nooksacks, for example, poled up and down their namesake river, often traveling as fast as 12 mph going upstream with two strong men tandem poling.

The idea is to place one end of a pole, normally 10 to 12 or even 14 feet long, into the river and, by pushing off the bottom, propel the craft in a given direction. It is done from a standing position in an open canoe and is far safer than it sounds. In fact, it is faster and more efficient for moving upstream than paddling, and it is an effective means of moving downstream as well. The Green River from the mouth of Soos Creek to Fort Dent Park, a run of 23 miles, has been poled in 6 hours, an average of roughly 4 mph on a relatively slow river.

Many of the rivers in this book are ideal for poling. Rocky bottoms full of huge angular blocks can be difficult because the pole may become entrapped between rocks and lost or bent (always carry along a paddle so you can retrieve a lost pole). Gravel bottoms are often good for poling unless the gravel is so loose that it offers no real purchase for the pole. Sand and mud bottoms may offer little resistance to the push of the pole and tend to grab the pole. Clay bottoms offer a firm surface to push off of, but they too tend to grab the pole at the withdrawal stage.

In water too deep for the pole to reach bottom (such as the lakelike stretch of the Black River and the big pools in many rivers described in this book), a kayak stroke can be used, simply paddling with the pole, which offers enough resistance to the water to provide plenty of power and control.

To begin poling, simply practice standing up in an open canoe, rocking it from side to side until comfortable with its stability. Try this on a lake or on a river with no visible current. Then start wielding the pole against the bottom or as a kayak paddle (see above). As the pole pushes off a shallow bottom, continue the push by "climbing" the pole with the hands pushing it farther and farther behind the craft. Recover the pole with a quick pool-cue move after a final power thrust against the bottom, and set the pole for another series.

Harry Rock, National Poling Champion in the 1980s, has written an excellent series of articles for *The American Canoeist* (Vol. X, No. 1, 2, 3). For further information, contact Harry Rock, Chairperson, National Poling Committee, 111 Oneida Avenue, North Plainfield, NJ 07060.

Preparation and Training

Preparation and training for running river trips can keep paddlers busy all year—reading about rivers, river-running skills, paddle technique in the off-season (if there is one); conditioning the mind and the body with regular mental and physical exercise, which might include pool sessions (practicing paddle technique); working on maintaining equipment and gear so that it is in good condition for the next river trip.

Physical conditioning is important so that paddlers don't get stiff and sore from each trip they make—or have a heart attack because they are not well-enough conditioned for the planned outing. Mental conditioning means that paddlers learn enough about the activity, the equipment they plan to use, and the river they plan to run so that they are intellectually ready, psychologically fit for the outing.

Of course, paddlers who run rivers every weekend throughout the year and belong to paddle clubs that have regular pool sessions already know all this; but such paddlers can always help others appreciate the need for such preparation and conditioning.

SAFETY TECHNIQUES

The most important safety technique is to be prepared—for anything and everything (then nothing will happen). To take a single river trip without everything needed for any emergency is to court disaster. Rivers are not treacherous in themselves; they only seem treacherous to people who don't know them. It is the inappropriate things that people do on and in rivers—such as launching without PFDs or without having adequate means of controlling the craft, and boating under the influence of drugs or alcohol—that give rivers a bad name as recreational resources.

Be prepared by wearing PFDs (personal flotation device), by using extra flotation in the craft, by learning some paddle skills before launch and practicing them regularly. Paddlers should get to know the river and what to expect of it before testing their luck and courage. They should know their own limitations and have enough sense to stay off the river when it is too high to run safely. Plan trips carefully, and keep an eye on the weather.

Once on a river, scout the potential problems: rapid, logjam, sweeper, low dam. Paddlers can normally avoid most obstacles by landing and lining (letting the craft down with a line from shore) or portaging (carrying the craft and gear around the problem). Take the safe route if there is a choice. Go in a group whenever possible, and help the group develop and practice safe techniques.

If paddlers capsize, they should keep calm. They may be shocked by the water temperature and surprised by the force of the current, but they should not panic. The PFDs will keep them afloat. They should keep their feet on the surface, facing downstream, and scull (like one would if sitting in an inner tube). And they should look for obstacles, such as logjams, rocks, sweepers, souse holes, or keepers (strong eddies in which the current is flowing strongly upstream), and try to avoid them.

When people go overboard, they should normally try immediately to get back to the boat. Few people fall out of canoes without the canoe's capsizing, but they do fall out of rafts and dories. If people are in the water for any length of time, they have three things to worry about: (1) getting caught between the craft and a natural obstacle; (2) getting caught by a natural obstacle such as a sweeper, keeper, or underwater snag that would tend to hold them in place, perhaps even underwater, a condition known as entrapment; and (3) hypothermia, the loss of too much body heat to cold water.

The worst obstacle could be the craft itself. Paddlers should move to the upstream end or side of the craft so it does not trap them between it and an obstacle in the river. It could crush paddlers or hold them in an untenable position with the force of the current and the weight of the river in the craft. Stay with the craft, which offers additional flotation and the chance of help, only if it seems the logical thing to do. It may make more sense to swim or wade to shore, but wade only in calm water.

If overboard paddlers are near shore in a logical place to get out of the water, they should go for it and leave the craft to its other occupants or to recover later. If the water is cold, they should get out as soon as they can do so safely, but they shouldn't try to stand in fast-moving water; feet can become entrapped in obstacles on the bottom. One of the best reasons to travel in a group is so there will be a support team ready to help in an emergency.

Hypothermia is the condition wherein so much body heat is lost that the body ceases to function normally. Early signs are shivering, blue lips, lethargy, then loss of small muscle coordination, and slurred speech. As soon as it is recognized, something must be done about it immediately: stop heat loss and warm the body by putting on warmer clothes or taking off wet clothes and putting on dry ones. Stop to build a fire if necessary and get high-energy foods and warm liquids into the victim (if the victim is conscious).

Remember in which direction safety lies. Is the road on this side of the river or across the river? As paddlers float any of these rivers, they should be aware of their location relative to access roads and railroad tracks, have an emergency game plan in mind outlining what to do in a variety of circumstances, and know the nearest route to safety and help. People are more important than equipment in the rescue priority. Get the people to safety before considering the craft, even though the craft may be expensive and a means of finishing the trip (the paddlers may not finish it at all if they get caught in a logjam). People have drowned by trying to retrieve gear after they were safely ashore.

Good paddle skills go a long way in keeping a party safe on the river, but so does common sense, sense enough not to go onto waters the party is not prepared to handle or into situations beyond the party's ability. Plan the trips. Gather information about the canoe routes. Read about them. Get the maps. Talk to people, especially people who know the river well and have run it recently.

When paddlers are on the river, they must keep their wits about them. Be observant. Look for problem areas. Anticipate problems. Talk to other boaters, fishermen, people along the river who might have better or more current information. Several people die on Washington rivers every year because they didn't know enough about the river to which they were entrusting their lives (like the boys who died at Canyon Falls in the summer of 1988).

Safety equipment is of little use unless used correctly. Someone on every river trip should know enough about first aid to use a first aid kit and to do the most basic things to provide appropriate assistance to a sick or injured person. CPR (cardiopulmonary resuscitation) is an important skill to have on any outdoor trip, especially on a river trip. CPR and first aid training should be a primary consideration for anyone planning regular river trips.

Most accidents on river trips actually happen off the river: driving to and from the river, loading and unloading crafts and gear, rigging boats, building campfires (including breaking firewood), and walking on sharp or slippery rocks at the river's edge. Be aware of the potential for accidents and anticipate the problems. Paddlers must watch where they step, how they lift, what they do and how they do it, especially if they are novices just learning the routine.

And develop a routine. There will be fewer mistakes and fewer accidents if a pattern is developed for everything that is done in the preparation for and execution of a river trip. Follow the pattern as it is perfected. There are so many things that can go wrong on a river trip that paddlers need to create a situation in which they control the circumstances as much as possible. Plan to the point of the ridiculous and follow the plan to the letter. Control what can be controlled, and the trip will be safer and more enjoyable.

Some clothing can weigh paddlers down beyond the capacity of their PFDs to buoy them up. Boots can fill with water and pull paddlers under. For such reasons a rain suit is a lot safer than a poncho, wet-suit boots a lot more sensible than pacs (rubber-bottomed waterproof boots).

There are two basic safety rules: **never boat alone** (that is, with only one boat; most polers do pole alone occasionally, especially when they pole upstream, for lack of anyone else who is into the activity) and **wear a PFD at all times on the river.** Sometimes these rules may seem unimportant on Class I and modest Class II water, but people have gotten themselves into serious trouble by not following them.

If paddlers go in a party, as they should to live by the rule of never boating alone, they may want to establish an order: Bob's boat leads because he knows the river best; Sam's goes next because he's the least experienced; Alice follows as sweep because she has the first aid kit and the most experience in general, even though she doesn't know this river as well. Formation may be broken occasionally, but as a general rule it makes sense to have some order.

A related rule is that no boat should ever get out of sight of the next boat. The lead boat doesn't run away from the laggards, and the laggards try to keep pace with the boats ahead. Tighten up the formation occasionally, as when approaching a riffle or a rapid. Scout rapids and troublesome areas that worry any of the boaters, and set up safety boats at critical points. All these suggestions are practiced by most paddle clubs. The use of safety throw lines (ropes stuffed in a bag that can be thrown to a person in the water or in an out-of-control craft) has become almost universal.

As mentioned earlier, one of the best ways to begin boating is to go with a paddle club. The members run safe and sane trips, and novice paddlers can learn the basics in a safe situation. Paddle clubs in western Washington include the following:

> **Paddle Trail Canoe Club**
> Box 24932, Seattle, WA 98124
> **Puget Sound Paddle Club**
> Box 22, Puyallup, WA 98371
> **Washington Kayak Club**
> Box 24264, Seattle, WA 98124
> (433-1983)
> **Washington Recreational River Runners**
> 1012 South 30th Court, Renton, WA 98055

In using this book remember that no rating system can be completely accurate or objective, that every river is different at different water levels, and that rivers can change from day to day, even hour to hour with tidal fluctuation or reservoir release flows. Logjams, sweepers and other obstacles can appear overnight due to natural conditions and human activity.

Some of the river segments in this book may have hazards that paddlers may feel are beyond their ability. A few of the rivers have

A Paddle Trail Canoe Club group stops for lunch.

special hazards, mentioned in the trip descriptions, that paddlers will want to portage or line—like the low dam on the Stillaguamish River (Trip 10) just downstream from the I-5 bridge. Paddlers can usually portage or line their craft around even massive logjams.

Paddlers should always be prepared on river trips and use their best judgment. Judgment will improve as the paddlers become more familiar with the rivers relative to the ratings in this book and with their own skills, abilities and confidences.

Use the ratings as a guide, not as an absolute. Nothing beats an examination of a potentially dangerous situation at the time and place that the condition exists.

THE NATURAL ENVIRONMENT

Nowhere except at sea or in the heart of the most pristine wilderness can the natural environment be experienced as meaningfully as on a river. It provides the very medium of travel, the fauna and flora that add immeasurably to the boater's enjoyment, and the geologic backdrop through which the boater moves.

Paddlers will observe many destructive aspects as they float these river segments—clear-cut scars, municipal and industrial pollution, dams that dewater, drown and destroy the natural environment, commercial development and exploitation that ignore and therefore abuse the natural environment—but they will also experience numerous positive elements of the natural world that may serve as inspiration and offer insights to act upon.

Aldo Leopold has said in essence that we abuse the land because we consider it a commodity that belongs to us; if we thought of it as a community to which we belong, which is closer to the truth, we might learn to use it with love and respect. No one can spend any length of time on a river without coming to better understand the natural environment and developing a higher respect for it. It behooves all paddlers to get their elected officials out on the rivers. There the elected officials can learn greater respect for the natural environment so that their future actions may stop the abuse of it and give it greater understanding.

The Character of the Medium

Rivers. By their very nature, rivers inspire awe. They are living beings with a life of their own. They nurture life, plant and animal. They flow toward the sea, seeking a dynamic equilibrium which they never reach. They erode the land, carving the features we see, the valleys and canyons, and they transport materials, organic and inorganic, creating new land in deltas and flood plains.

They are bound by their bottoms and their shorelines, but those boundaries change. Flood waters scour the river bottoms and inundate pastures, farmlands and other low-lying areas. Where mankind has been foolish enough to build in the floodplain, we hear of the treacherous rivers that have caused damage to human property or taken human life, as though humans are all that matters. (Will humans ever learn not to build in the floodplain?)

Watercraft float on the surface of the rivers, displacing a small amount of water for the time they are on the river, leaving no evidence of their passing—unless the paddlers are careless and insensitive and have left their litter and human waste behind.

The rivers provide the power for the float trips, the paddle parties. Boaters may control their crafts, augment the downhill speed of the river or buck it for a time with pole, paddle or oar, but ultimately it is the river that rules. Boaters need to learn to go with the flow, to listen to and sense the river's messages. Unless people learn to read the river, they will never know its secrets.

Estuaries. The richest sources of life on the planet are estuaries. They are the areas where freshwater rivers meet the salt sea. The natural mixing that occurs, augmented by the twice-daily tidal stirring,

Mount Baker and the Twin Sisters rising over Bellingham Bay.

creates a unique habitat used by thousands of species. Twice each day the estuary and the lower reaches of the rivers that feed it are flushed by the tide, cleansed of the waste products of life that are then recycled, even as the waters themselves are recycled in the hydrologic cycle.

Boating on estuaries and in the tidal reaches of rivers requires an understanding of the tides, their ebb and flow. Boaters have to work with the tides; they are stronger than the boaters. Estuaries offer a unique opportunity to see several worlds. Think of it: at high tide people see only the full flood of the estuary, but at low tide people get a glimpse of the muddy, sandy or rocky bottom and of the organisms that have been covered by the swirling waters of the natural mixing bowl.

Estuaries are full of bird life: eagles, wintering snow geese and swans, summer resident ducks and shorebirds, spring and fall migrants. But so are they rich in mammals, from an occasional whale to seals and, along the shore, beaver and muskrats, deer and raccoons. They are vital feeding grounds for juvenile anadromous (freshwater-born ocean-feeding) fish.

Boaters need to be aware of the differences tides make in these productive estuaries: the swift currents that are generated, that fluctuate, that swirl in lateral loops; the mud flats left behind when the tide goes out; the fogs generated when river water meets saltwater at different temperatures; the difficulty of paddling or rowing against the tide. In the estuaries, more than anywhere else on the river, boaters have an opportunity to feel the pulse of the earth in its waters.

Natural History

The fauna and flora of rivers offer enough material to keep the most ardent river runner curious and mentally stimulated for a lifetime. Rivers teem with life; their bottoms serve as habitat for invertebrates, and the invertebrates feed the fish and amphibians as well as many of the birds (such as the water ouzel, which flies under water seeking its insect diet).

Fishermen try to "match the hatch" of insects on the river, fly fishing for adult salmonoids while kingfishers and great blue herons fish for the fry. Bald eagles and osprey nest along the rivers and feed on larger fish; the eagles especially congregate in midwinter to scavenge the spawned-out salmon. Spring warblers flood the rivers with their songs and nest along the banks in summer. Spotted sandpipers and killdeer frequent

Canada geese rest on a Snohomish River gravel bar.

the river bars; ducks—mallards, mergansers, harlequins, golden-eyes—nest and feed as well.

Because rivers are open, it is possible to see from the boat many woodland species of wildlife, especially birds—western tanagers, black-headed grosbeaks, flycatchers, robins, warblers. Several species of swallows feed on the insect population over the rivers, and the raven is rarely far away. Many meadow-dwelling birds can be seen and heard from the river as they conduct their courtship, including meadowlarks and Washington's state bird, the goldfinch. Birds enliven any river trip.

The natural habitat along rivers, even in developed areas, has continued to support wildlife. Few of the rivers in this book would be considered wild in any sense, but all of them—even Sammamish Slough—have beaver and muskrats. All of them have runs of anadromous fish. Many of them have deer and coyotes; a few have bear. Most of the rivers on the Olympic Peninsula have elk; many have otter, mink, skunks, raccoon, squirrels and rabbits. All of them provide natural habitat for a great variety of birds.

The explosion of Mount St. Helens did much to make people aware of geological phenomena. In western Washington virtually every geological process known to humankind goes on, from the carving of the landscape by glaciers and rivers to the results of plate tectonics—earthquakes and volcanoes. Rivers continually carve the land, continually deposit the materials they carry down from the mountains to the lowlands. On river trips boaters can see it all happening. In fact, as boaters come to understand geological phenomena better, they will understand what makes a river do what it does in its search for dynamic equilibrium.

River running gets people outdoors onto the rivers where the natural world functions, following immutable natural laws. Paddlers learn to observe, wonder about things, learn how they fit together and interact with one another. Paddling a river offers a course in ecology, an opportunity to see how the natural world works. (Get your political representatives out on the rivers so they may learn too.)

Conservation

Conservation has been defined in many ways, but essentially it is the antithesis of wastefulness. Anything that causes waste fails to function naturally, for there is no waste in natural systems; everything is used. Natural systems are based on recycling. So far, humans merely dabble in recycling, while using technology to create massive quantities of waste products that cannot be used by natural systems. And so far, humans have not been able to find enough places to dispose of or to store these waste products.

River users—boaters, fishermen, picnickers, campers, whoever—have an opportunity to leave the natural world in as natural a state as possible. Unless they are totally thoughtless, careless and ignorant, passing boaters should have little impact on the waters they travel or on the adjacent lands. The swirl of water caused by paddles and oars creates little impact, and even the noise level can be controlled in muscle-powered crafts if boaters are sensitive and sensible.

All outdoor users have a moral responsibility to leave the natural world as pristine as they find it and to improve it when necessary by picking up the litter others have left. Just as only humans can prevent forest fires, only humans—all of us—can prevent the deterioration of the natural environment by treating it with love and respect.

There is no need to clear natural vegetation away to make a campsite or picnic area more comfortable. There is no need to cut living trees or scar their trunks or cut their limbs or mutilate shrubs or pick wildflowers. When these things are done, these parts of our natural world are no longer there for others to enjoy. There is no need to leave ugly fire pits, scars and ashes on a river beach; boaters can cook on camp stoves or carry out the ashes and charcoal the fires produce. Most paddle clubs participate in annual river clean-ups, joining with other river users to maintain the waterways in as natural a state as possible.

The old admonition to take nothing but pictures, leave nothing but footprints—and not too many of them—makes a lot of sense to the sensitive; and the insensitive have no business in the natural world but destruction. The environmentally aware—and that is more of us every day—frequently join together to coordinate efforts, to think globally but act locally.

These statewide, regional and national conservation and environmental organizations can use your help, and they can help you as well:

American Rivers
    801 Pennsylvania Avenue SE
    Suite 303
    Washington, DC 20008

American Wilderness Alliance
    7600 E. Arapahoe Road
    Suite 114
    Englewood, CO 80112

National Wildlife Federation
    1400 Sixteenth Street NW
    Washington, DC 20036-2266

Friends of the Earth
    218 D Street SE
    Washington, DC 20003

National Audubon Society
    950 Third Avenue
    New York, NY 10022

Northwest Rafters Association
P.O. Box 19008
Portland, OR 97219

Rivers Council of Washington
1731 Westlake Avenue N., Suite 202
Seattle, WA 98109-3043

River Network
P.O. Box 8787
Portland, OR 97207

Sierra Club
730 Polk Street
San Francisco, CA 94109

The Izaak Walton League
1401 Wilson Blvd.
Level B
Arlington, VA 22209

The Mountaineers
300 3rd Avenue W.
Seattle, WA 98119

The Nature Conservancy
217 Pine Street, #1100
Seattle, WA 98101

The Wilderness Society
1400 I Street NW
10th Floor
Washington, DC 20006-2596

Washington Environmental Council
1100 2nd Avenue, #102
Seattle, WA 98010

The National Wild and Scenic Rivers System

The National Wild and Scenic Rivers System was established in 1968 by an act of Congress, which established a national policy of preserving from development and exploitation certain rivers and their adjacent environments. It also established a method for evaluating rivers and adding them to that system. Initially there were only eight rivers in the system.

At this writing, there are 153 Wild and Scenic rivers in the nation, several of them in western Washington: the Skagit; its tributaries the

Cascade and the Sauk; a Sauk tributary, the Suiattle; and two Columbia River tributaries, the White Salmon and the Klickitat.

In 1988 the President's Commission on Americans Outdoors recommended that by the year 2000 the United States set aside for protective designation 2,000 rivers nationwide. There is a long ways to go to reach that goal. Several western Washington rivers have been proposed for protection, including a number on the Olympic Peninsula. So far, this has been prevented from happening. It may be time for Washingtonians to do a little of their own thinking in the realm of preserving rivers.

Oregon recently added 40 of its rivers to the national system and doubled its state system from 11 to 22 protected rivers. Washington, with more rivers, has only a small fraction of rivers protected from exploitation. A grass-roots movement has begun among paddlers and fishermen in the state to change that fact and to add several Washington rivers to the federal system.

More than half of the states have their own scenic rivers programs. Washington is one of those states, but it has only one river in its program, the Skykomish, and the designation is largely meaningless. It names part of the Skykomish as a state scenic river but gives it virtually no protection. Is Oregon so rich that it can offer significant protection to more than 20 state designated rivers and more than 40 federally designated? Are we so poor that we can't?

The state legislature has taken some encouraging action in recent legislative sessions toward enlarging the State Scenic Waterways System, but if every paddler in the state gets involved, Washington can become a leader in river protection.

RIVER ETIQUETTE

River etiquette refers to manners on the river. It has nothing to do with rules or regulations, liabilities or laws; it involves common sense and sensitivity to others—on the river, on the shore, at campsites and picnic areas, at put-ins and take-outs. It includes respect for private property and public property, for wildlife and the natural environment, and for other people. In essence it involves following the golden rule: do unto others as you would have them do unto you. It is a matter of following conventions, of practicing common-sense thoughtfulness. It can be applied in many ways:

■ If boaters would like to have a clean place to camp or stop for lunch, they should clean up their own campsite or lunch stop area when they leave (it will be clean for the next party, and it may encourage them to follow a pattern that will benefit all river users);

■ If boaters want a quiet, peaceful river trip, they shouldn't play the boom box on the river (in fact, they shouldn't even bring it along) or practice loud raucous behavior on the river;

■ If boaters want the privilege of launching from or stopping at someone's private property, they should ask permission first and then keep the property clean;

■ If boaters want to be treated with respect by fishermen, they should treat fishermen with respect (they shouldn't spoil their fishing by paddling over their fishing hole or slaloming their lines);

■ If boaters want a natural river, they shouldn't spoil it with litter or soap suds or apple cores or orange peelings.

Just be a decent human being. Ask permission to use private property or tribal lands; follow regulations where and when they exist; use common sense.

Beginning at the beginning, boaters should take up as little time and space as possible at the put-in. They should be well enough organized and sensitive to other boaters and other river users so that they don't intrude upon anyone else's space or time.

On the river be aware of other boaters and other river users including fishermen in and on the water. Boaters should ask how they can least disturb fishermen by going to the left or right of them. Don't crowd other boats or intrude on groups of boaters; do not engage them in water fights or otherwise disturb their experience.

Paddlers should not intrude on other parties stopped for lunch or to camp, but they should be courteous and responsive. The other party may appreciate the insights and expertise of another river user. But thoughtful river users won't overstay their welcome.

At the take-out, move quickly off the ramp and out of the way of other river users. Consolidate gear, and as at the put-in, take up as little time and space as possible. Don't rush, but conversely, don't loiter.

And don't litter. Trash and garbage, bottles and cans don't belong in the river or on its banks. River users should carry out their own debris so no one else has to clean up after them. In fact, boaters can help clean up after others less careful and sensitive, thereby leaving the river a better place than before.

When it comes to private property, do not trespass. The waters of the state are public, but their shorelines may not be. To be safe, assume that the banks of all rivers are in private ownership. Some, of course, are public lands: public parks, Department of Natural Resource (DNR) lands, Department of Wildlife properties, and highway rights of way (the area under bridges is generally public land).

Ask permission to use someone's private access, picnic area or campsite. Know that the river below mean high water mark is usually public land, but some old railroad rights of way may not be. Don't press the point with an irate landowner. Because of the popularity of steelhead fishing in western Washington, state agencies have acquired river access in numerous places. Such access points are generally marked on the sketch maps in this book (if they are reliable and accessible). These

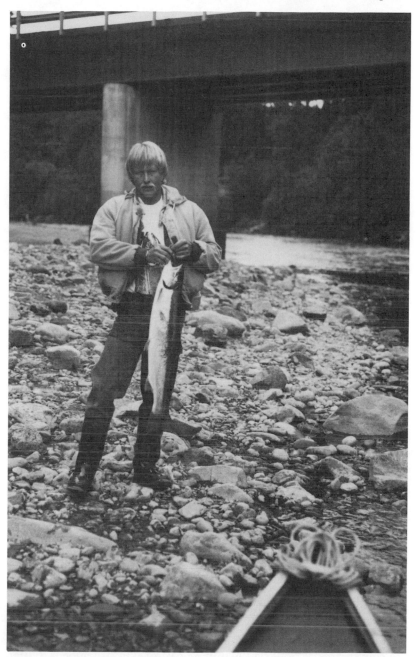

A steelhead fisherman with his first catch of the day.

Tubers float the Nooksack's South Fork beneath the Twin Sisters.

require a conservation, fishing or hunting license for each user. They are not free to the general public.

Indian lands are a special kind of private property. Some tribes welcome boaters, especially those in human-muscle-powered crafts, but others discourage non-Indian boaters on the reservations or require a special license or guide. Ask permission to use the rivers that flow through Indian lands, and respect the tribal decision. Be sure to go through the tribal authority; an individual tribal member might grant permission and another tribal member might take exception to the permission granted. Stick to official channels.

Public access is a big issue on some rivers: the Humptulips, for example. A favorite steelhead fishing river, it once had numerous access points on private lands, but many of them were recently closed by landowners on the Humptulips in a political power-play growing out of the county's restrictions on the mining of gravel in streambeds. Other landowners have closed their property to boaters due to litter problems. It pays to be a good neighbor on the river.

TIDES

A number of the river segments discussed in this book involve saltwater tidal areas, the lower reaches of rivers and their mouths that are impacted by twice-daily tides. Yet there is another kind of tide that boaters must consider; the rising and falling tides of reservoir-release rivers.

Any dammed river will be impacted by the flows released from its upstream dams. This is especially evident on the Skagit and the Cowlitz rivers but to some extent also on the Cedar, Green, Nisqually and Wynoochee rivers. Be sure to read any posted warnings and check the river-flow information available on NOAA's hotline (526-8530).

Pacific Ocean tides are different from Puget Sound tides, which vary from north to south and with the distance from the Strait of Juan de Fuca. The Columbia River is impacted by both reservoir releases from upstream dams and from the Pacific Ocean tidal flow,which impacts the river's lower tributaries (only the Gray's River/Seal Slough/Deep River complex covered in this book).

In running many of these segments, boaters need to understand a few basic facts about tides. There are two high tides and two low tides each day (most days); one of each is higher than the other. The four tides are known as higher high water, lower high water, higher low water, and lower low water. Make sense? The height of the tide is measured in feet above mean lower low water (zero). A higher high water of 6.0 following a lower low water of 2.0 means a fluctuation of 8 vertical feet.

Since the tidal (lunar) day is roughly 50 minutes longer than the solar day, the tides alter by nearly an hour each day, becoming later and later until they advance to early the next day. It is important to differentiate between tides and tidal currents. Tides are indicated by the high and low vertical rising and falling of the water; tidal currents are the horizontal movements of the water as the tides fluctuate. Ebb is the seaward movement of water; flood is the inward (landward) movement.

Slack water occurs after the tides change, that is, after they reach their high or low point. That time varies with several factors and can rarely be judged exactly for a given point; barometric pressure, wind direction and velocity all alter actual on-site tide levels, and any constriction in the flow of the tide may slightly alter its level in a given area. It may take an hour or two in some areas before a paddler can really tell what the tide is doing.

That's why it is important to gather as much information as possible before trying tidal areas. Both tide and current tables are useful in calculating the height of the tide or its ultimate ebb. Detailed tide and tidal current tables published annually by the National Ocean Survey are available at most nautical supply stores and a few boating shops. For best information, use nautical charts in conjunction with tide and current tables to judge the specific tide levels for the desired river mouth.

The pocket-sized tide table booklets available from many fishing and boating retailers as an advertising tool or at a nominal cost are useful, but they say little about currents; nor do they give very specific information about the time it takes the tide to turn in a given area.

Most of the river segments described in this book involve only minimal tidal paddling, but saltwater reaches where currents are strong can be dangerous. The maximum danger is normally at minimal tide, that is, at the greatest ebb, when the draw-down of the tide is accentuated by the flow of the river. The currents under such circumstances, especially in shallow water and in constricted areas, can be violent. Avoid such areas at such times by consulting tide, and if possible, current tables.

MAPS AND CHARTS

Maps (USGS) and charts (NOAA) where available are suggested for each river segment in this book, but they will do little good unless paddlers know (or learn) how to read them. Sketch maps are also provided for every river segment in the book. Each map is oriented to be read traveling downstream. That is, the top of the map is downstream; the bottom is the upstream starting point. Directions such as "river left" or "river right" and references to the left or right bank also are based on a downstream-facing orientation.

River miles (RM) are measured from the mouth of the river. Thus on the Stillaguamish, the main stem is measured from where it flows into Port Susan. Since the South Fork is considered the river's main stem, the river mile measurements on the South Fork above its confluence with the North Fork continue to climb in sequence. But the North Fork mileage begins at the confluence (that is, at the mouth of the North Fork) which is its RM 0.

In some cases a river will split around an island or into a series of sloughs (the Snohomish, for example) and the diifferent channels or sloughs will vary in length. The main channel is given the official total mileage. If, for example, the distance around an island is 2 miles by the main channel and 2.3 by the other, the accumulated distance to the head of the island from the tip will be 2 miles, not 2.3 miles.

The sketch maps, which include river miles, show only the basic details that help locate the take-out and put-in points and alternate accesses. In a few cases an adjacent map helps identify the shuttle route.

The most detailed maps are USGS topographic maps, available from some local map stores, a few paddle shops and the U.S. Geological Survey (Box 25286 Federal Center, Denver, CO 80225). Although 7.5′ maps are more detailed, for some of the river segments in this book, only 15' maps are available. However, USGS maps may not show the rivers as well as the maps found in the *Catalog of Washington Streams and Salmon Utilization,* published by the Washington Department of Fisheries in 1975 (the road information on these maps is less reliable; many of the road names and numbers have been changed).

Local chambers of commerce and some commercial establishments produce fairly reliable area maps that may be useful in finding river accesses (Grays Harbor map of Aberdeen, Hoquiam and Cosmopolis, for example, covers important accesses for four river segments). Milt Keizer's *Complete Handbook on Washington Steelheading* (1988) includes reasonably accurate maps showing river access points. Many parks and recreation agencies produce good maps that include river access points (for example, 11 river segments in this book can be followed on the King County Parks and Recreation map).

County maps published by the Washington Department of Transportation (Public Transportation and Planning, Highway Administration Building. Olympia, WA 98504) show rivers in reasonable detail and provide the off-river background needed to follow the shuttle routes. The commercial map of Washington State recently published by DeLorme Mapping Company is also very useful.

Official charts from the National Oceanic and Atmospheric Administration (NOAA) can be obtained from two Seattle offices—the 13th Coast Guard District Office in the Federal Building (915 2nd Avenue, Seattle, WA 98174-1067) and the National Ocean Service Office (1801 Fairview Avenue E, Seattle, WA 98102)—or from the Distribution Branch, (N/CG33), National Ocean Service, Riverdale, MD 20737-1199, or numerous commercial retail outlets (with less hassle).

NOAA produces and markets tide tables, tidal current tables, tidal current charts and tidal current diagrams to help paddlers keep safe on the tidal reaches of the rivers. Paddlers may gather more information than they ever really wanted to know if they simply order the tables, charts and diagrams they might think they need, and the cost will add up. Study what is available and have a clerk explain the various documents before spending a lot of money on something that isn't really needed. An index of Pacific Coast charts is free for the asking.

THE TRIPS

Dakota Creek at low tide.

1 DAKOTA CREEK/ CALIFORNIA CREEK

Location: near Blaine, northwest of Bellingham
Distance: 1 to 3 miles each creek
River Time: 2 to 3 hours each creek
Map: Blaine (7.5'); NOAA Chart: 18421
Best Season: all year
Hazards: tides, wind on the saltwater
Shuttle: 5 miles at most on paved roads, but no shuttle needed
Rating: A, T

Overview. Dakota Creek and California Creek both flow into Drayton Harbor just south of the U.S.-Canada border. The harbor created by Semiahmoo Spit is well protected for canoe and kayak paddling. Its mud flats offer excellent bird watching, and the harbor provides fine views of Mount Baker and the nearby Canadian peaks. The creeks themselves allow access to amazing wildlife habitat for so urban an area. This is a quiet trip through a riverside community, a mix of majestic old homes and new condominiums that blend well into the picturesque surroundings.

Access. The easiest access, both launch site and take-out, is at Semiahmoo Park on the spit. From this put-in, paddlers can make a round trip by water, 2 miles each way, to the mouth of either creek and back (no land shuttle). The creek mouths are several hundred yards apart, but at low tide a mud flat will force a detour of more than a mile between the two.

An alternate starting (and ending) point is the left bank of California Creek at its mouth, just west of the California Creek bridge on Drayton Harbor Road. There is very limited shoulder parking here. If this access is used, it is best to arrange a shuttle for an exit pickup rather than to leave a car parked at the access. The mouth of Dakota Creek can be reached from here by paddling across the eastern edge of the harbor.

A third and less desirable but frequently used access that avoids the saltwater approach is a rough put-in on Dakota Creek under the Burlington Northern railroad bridge southwest of the Old Highway 99 bridge.

Driving Directions. Take Exit 274 off I-5 3 miles south of the U.S.-Canada border, head toward Old Highway 99, then turn south onto Blaine Road. Half a mile after crossing the Dakota Creek bridge, turn

51

right onto Drayton Harbor Road, (almost immediately you will cross California Creek) and follow it westward along the southern edge of Drayton Harbor to Semiahmoo Drive (from the left), turn right to Semiahmoo Spit and Whatcom County Park. Park here and launch onto the bay on the east side of the spit.

For access at the mouth of California Creek, pull off to the right on Drayton Harbor Road less than 100 yards after crossing California Creek—just after the turnoff from Blaine Road.

To find the Dakota Creek access, head southeast on Old Highway 99 from the I-5 exit mentioned above. The access is reached by parking on the right shoulder, on the west side of the road, north of the bridge across Dakota Creek, then bushwhacking along a faint trail between the highway and the railroad tracks down to the north bank of Dakota Creek. Since it is a tough haul back up, it may make sense to plan a take-out at the mouth of California Creek, a 1-mile shuttle, round trip, or on Semiahmoo Spit, a 5-mile shuttle (see above).

A logjam on Dakota Creek.

DAKOTA CREEK, CALIFORNIA CREEK

Loomis Trail Road

DAKOTA CREEK

CALIFORNIA CREEK

Railroad

Burlington Northern

③

②

⑤

③

②

①

99

①

Alternate Start/End

Exit 274

Blaine Road

Drayton

Alternate Start/End

Washington
British Columbia

DRAYTON HARBOR

Harbor

Road

Blaine

START/END

Miles
0   1

Semiahmoo Park

Semiahmoo Drive

DAKOTA CREEK/CALIFORNIA CREEK

Description. The navigable portions of both creeks are tidal. A good way to explore them is by paddling (or poling) upstream with the incoming tide, then following the outgoing tide back to the harbor. The eastern portion of the harbor is shallow, a mud flat exposed at low tide, forcing paddlers who would explore both rivers in one day to detour out into the harbor at low tide, not an altogether unpleasant experience because of the birdlife on the mud flats and the marine life in the water (including migrating salmon during certain seasons). Bottom fish and crabs scurry along the eelgrass, and shorebirds—spotted sandpipers, dunlins, sanderlings, wandering tattlers—feed on the exposed mud flats.

Dakota Creek flows primarily with the tide, except during heavy rains, and the tidal flow is strong. The riverbed is virtually unnavigable at low tide. The lower reaches of the creek are developed. There is a shipyard near the mouth, then several bridges—Blaine Road, the Burlington Northern Railroad, Old 99, then the double spans of I-5—and finally homes set back from the creek. Within half a mile, the creek narrows, wilderness begins to encroach upon the stream, and the experience becomes more intimate.

Barnacles encrust logs and dock pilings, even living trees, and there are raccoon tracks, deer in the flesh, great blue herons, nesting Canada geese. Boreal birds abound. There are high grassy banks where geese rest in the summer sun; blackberry bushes festooned with fresh fruit in the late summer and early fall hang over the creek. Chamomile, smelling like pineapple, grows wild, ready to be picked for tea.

Forge up the creek as far as the tide or fallen trees will allow, stop for lunch on one of the grassy banks, and let the tide turn. Then return to the harbor with the pull of the tide. Explore the other creek—or call it a day.

California Creek is broader than Dakota Creek in its lower reaches. Seals occasionally follow fish into the tidal basin just above the bridge at the mouth of California Creek. Numerous waterfowl congregate here as well. Flanked by new condominiums that are soon left behind, the lower creek quickly gives way to more open country and occasional views of Mount Baker.

The creek curves, crossed by low bridges, flanked by Loomis Trail roads. Channelized in earlier days, it flows almost straight for a couple of miles. It is more open than Dakota Creek, more developed; but geese and gulls are here, as well as ducks and raptors. Deer and raccoon visit at dawn and dusk, and the great blue heron is always nearby.

Even though roads cross and parallel California Creek, paddling on its tidal waters offers an opportunity to get away from the work-a-day world. An early-morning run of either creek can be day-breaking glorious, and a late-afternoon trip may reward the paddler with a spectacular sunset.

Lummi River, with Mount Baker in the background.

2 *LUMMI RIVER*

Location: Lummi Indian Reservation northwest of Bellingham
Distance: 3 miles
River Time: 1 to 2 hours
Map: Lummi Bay (7.5'); NOAA Charts: 18423, 18424
Best Season: all year, best birding in winter
Hazards: low water, tides, man-made debris
Shuttle: 6 miles at most on paved and gravel roads, but no shuttle
needed
Rating: A, T

Overview. The Lummi River, marked "Red River" on some maps, is a high-water overflow channel of the Nooksack River. Channelized and diked, it may be an unappealing river at first glance, but it makes an excellent birdwatching trip, especially in the winter, when it has everything from snowy owls and both trumpeter and whistling swans to peregrine falcons and bald eagles, a dozen species of ducks and both Canada and snow geese. It offers views of Mount Baker and the

Canadian peaks and refreshing winds off the Strait of Georgia. *Note:* Permission to boat the Lummi River must be obtained from the Lummi Indian Tribal Council, 2616 Kwina Road, Bellingham, WA 98225, or call 206-734-8180.

Access. Either put-in or take-out points are continuous for most of its length from adjacent roads that parallel the river; North Red River Road and South Red River Road on opposite sides of the Lummi River. It is possible to launch a lightweight boat almost anywhere along the runnable route, but the unpaved lower end of South Red River Road is badly choked with tall weeds in summer and early fall, making access difficult.

Driving Directions. To reach the Lummi River take Highway 540 off I-5 (Exit 260) and travel west on Slater Road to Haxton Way. Turn left (south) on Haxton to North Red River Road, and turn right—or cross the Lummi River and turn right onto South Red River Road (the two roads embrace the river). Access to the river can be made from either road.

Description. The Lummi River, named for the Lummi Indian Tribe on whose lands the river flows for all of its runnable course, offers many fine views of Mount Baker and of the Canadian peaks to the north. It flows through open country, for the most part, with its upper reaches bordered by thickets. Wintering snow geese and trumpeter and whistling swans utilize the area, as do numerous raptorial species; it is a birdwatcher's paradise.

This can easily be a round-trip river; no shuttle is necessary if tide charts are consulted and followed. Launch near the junction of Haxton Road with either of the river-flanking roads and paddle southwestward past muskrat dens, nesting ducks, feeding pheasants, soaring raptors and fishing great blue heron. A model-airplane flying field lies on the left bank in the first mile; don't be surprised to see and hear a variety of miniature planes.

Unfortunately some of the riverbank has been used as a dumping ground; there are unsightly areas especially along the upper reaches of this small river. But its tidal waters are delightful, despite the fact that the river is diked. The Lummi delta attracts numerous species of bay ducks, waterfowl and shorebirds, and great blue herons and bald eagles often vie for perching places among the pilings remaining from decaying developments along the shoreline.

Blackberries cover much of the dike, offering succulent snacks during the late summer and early fall.Winter birding is ideal, but spring migrants also stop along the Lummi. On windy days or when the tide is turning, the delta can be dangerous, but its many channels and small bays still offer relatively protected paddling.

Pilings along the Nooksack protect the bank from erosion.

3 NOOKSACK RIVER: Everson to Lynden

Location: north of Bellingham
Distance: 8.5 miles to Lynden, 18 miles to Ferndale
River Time: 70 minutes to Lynden, 3 hours to Ferndale
Maps: Lawrence, Suma, Lynden, Bertrand Creek, Ferndale (7.5'),
*   Lynden (15')*
Best Season: all year, except at flood stage
Hazards: fast, cold water, logjams, sweepers
Shuttle: 8.1 miles to Lynden, 22 miles to Ferndale on paved roads
Rating: B+

Overview. The Nooksack River below the confluence of its major
forks is a cold, swift river that can be dangerous even to experienced
paddlers. Coming off the glaciers on Mount Baker, the river is usually
milky in summer and fall due to the glacial flour it carries. Often clear
in midwinter, it offers the finest views of Mount Baker of any river in
this book.This segment flows through farmlands where the smells of
berries, new-mown hay, silage and manure mingle with the river
smells (from spawned-out salmon in late fall to fresh mountain snow-
melt in spring).

Access. While there is excellent access beneath the bridge on Highway 542 near Cedarville from the east side of the river at RM 31, the river downstream has rambunctious tendencies that might intimidate some paddlers. From a limited-parking pullout on Highway 544 between Everson and Strandell there is access beneath the railroad bridge on the left (south) bank at RM 23.8. Below this point the river behaves itself better.

From here downstream the river is fast, but broad enough to allow paddlers ample room to maneuver around and away from obstacles.While there are several possible access points in the next few miles, a public fishing access (RM 15.3) off Meridian Road (Highway 539) southwest of Lynden offers a good take-out for paddle craft, although it has no boat ramp.

For parties who want a longer run, the river is much the same to Ferndale, another 9.5 miles downstream. There is a new (1988) well-developed access with a boat ramp just south of Ferndale (RM 5.8), which—from the Everson put-in—makes an 18-mile run. At this river's rate of flow, that is still an easy day's run.

Driving Directions. For a take-out at Ferndale, use the Ferndale exit off I-5 (Exit 262) and head southwest. Just before reaching the Nooksack River bridge, turn left onto Hovander Road, then turn right almost immediately into the public fishing access jointly funded by the Whatcom County Parks Department and the Washington Department of Wildlife.

For the take-out on Highway 539 southwest of Lynden, take Highway 539 north out of Bellingham (I-5 Exit 256) to the public fishing access immediately south of the river. An alternate approach is to take the Birch Bay–Lynden Road exit east off I-5 (Exit 270) northwest of Bellingham; at Highway 539, several miles east, turn right and drive the 1.5 miles to the public fishing access mentioned above, immediately south of the river.

For the launch site at Everson, take Highway 539 north from this public fishing access to Front Street; turn right into Lynden and head east through town, taking Hampton Road toward Hampton, a tiny town north of Everson. At Trap Line Road, turn right and follow it south to the river, turning left onto Main Street in Everson, then right, onto Highway 544, which crosses the river.

The parking area is on the right (west) side of the southbound lane immediately southwest of the bridge. Achieving river access involves crossing the northbound lane of traffic and following a steep use-maintained trail between the road and the railroad bridge to the river. The put-in is on the left bank of the river under either of the bridges (highway or railroad), depending on how the last high water has distributed the sand, silt and debris.

Description. The main Nooksack is cold and swift, a gray river even in summer under blue skies. Its high rating is due primarily to the fact that mishaps on the main Nooksack may have serious consequences because of the fast-flowing cold water. When it has less glacial flour— during winter and spring—it has a lovely greenish hue. The speed of the current is remarkable; at moderate water levels paddlers can average 7 miles per hour without really trying.

The river meanders among gravel islands through agricultural land where head-high corn and berry fields (blueberries, raspberries, strawberries) line the bank, and the smell of fresh cut hay mingles with the odor of animal waste. A dairy barn appears, a farmhouse, a wall of close-set pilings to deflect the river. Wild blackberries grow along the river bank, and foxgloves, tansy and Queen Anne's lace enliven the shoreline with their voluntary blossoms.

Tractor sounds mingle with bird songs and the music of the river. Goldfinches (Washington's state bird), crows, song sparrows, red-winged blackbirds, red-tailed hawks, spotted sandpipers, robins, great blue herons and several species of swallows populate the river in midsummer. Cottonwoods, willows and alders make up the taller vegetation.

More barns and houses appear, a few retaining walls of rip-rap and pilings protect the banks from erosion, especially at high water. There are logs and snags in the river (potential hazards), vast gravel bars, and good bird habitat. One canoeist finds "the easy [parts of the] Nooksack not scenic enough, but the birding potential is high." But so is the potential for views of Mount Baker; and the riverine environment, while not wilderness, offers much to enjoy, not the least of which is the fast-flowing current.

4 *NOOKSACK RIVER: South Fork*

Location: south of Deming (Saxon to Van Zandt vicinity)
Distance: 8 to 11 miles
River Time: 3 to 4 hours
Maps: Acme, Deming (7.5')
Best Season: late spring, early summer
Hazards: logjams, sweepers, high water
Shuttle: 8.1 and 10.6 miles on paved roads
Rating: B

Overview. The Nooksack's South Fork, a perfect river for tubing or canoeing, parallels Highway 9. The spectacular tips of the Twin Sisters can be seen from the river, and while the course of the river flows through farmlands, much of it is well wooded. There are riffles and mild rapids, temporary challenges to boaters, with few serious consequences except at high water. The South Fork is clear, the warmest of the three Nooksack forks, and offers good practice for more challenging runs elsewhere.

Access. The best put-in is at a bridge on Saxon Road about 1.5 miles southeast of Saxon at a wading and picnic spot that is a summer favorite among local residents. The launch site is from a sandy beach immediately upstream from the bridge on river right.

The best take-out is off Strand Road between Acme and Van Zandt, a public access area with a huge sand-and-gravel beach, the most popular summer recreation area in the whole valley.

An alternate take-out is the road right-of-way beneath the Potter Road bridge just west of Van Zandt. However, this is a relatively poor place to take out because the only parking is along the narrow roadside.

There is access near the mouth of the South Fork on a huge gravel bar at the confluence beneath the Highway 9 bridge across the main Nooksack. However, this access often requires a 4-wheel-drive vehicle because of the rough access road, and it may mean a long carry from the right bank of the South Fork, which can be steep and unstable at some water levels.

Driving Directions. To reach the put-in, turn east off Highway 9 about 2 miles south of Acme, onto Saxon Road. Travel 2.1 miles (passing through Saxon) to a bridge across the South Fork, where the paving ends. There is limited roadside parking here. Park east of the bridge (the road is gravel) if possible and carry the craft down to the right bank of the river immediately upstream of the bridge.

To reach any of three possible take-outs, return to Highway 9 and head north through Acme. The river flows beneath the highway just north of Acme and continues northward on the west side of the road for the remainder of this run. About 3 miles north of Acme (2 miles south of Van Zandt), turn left (west) on Strand Road and drive to its end, a popular local summer sunning and picnicking area with a broad beach, an ideal take-out for an 8-mile run.

The second possibility, which involves an additional 3 miles on the river, is a roadside take-out beneath the bridge just west of Van Zandt. To reach this less-desirable access, drive north to Van Zandt, turning left (west) onto Potter Road. There is only roadside parking here with private property on both sides; only the road right-of-way allows access.

A third possibility is to run all the way to the mouth of the South Fork, another 2 miles (total from the put-in, 13 miles). Since the main

Logjams and low water levels narrow the South Fork of the Nooksack.

Nooksack is extremely swift here, a good Class III river, be sure to beach before reaching the confluence. Access is on river right, where there is a huge gravel bar accessible from Highway 9 by a dirt (or mud) road that is often extremely rough. The turn off is on the west side of Highway 9 (between the highway and the railroad tracks) about 200 yards south of the bridge across the main Nooksack.

Description. The South Fork is shallow in summer, clear and delightful, full of tubing teenagers on a warm sunny day. The river may flow through agricultural land, but the farms are unobtrusive, shielded by forest. These same forests no doubt contribute to the extensive debris in the river. There are logjams, sweepers and snags—occasionally trees all the way across the river—that could be problems

NOOKSACK RIVER, SOUTH FORK

To Deming

1

Alternate Take-out

Alternate Take-out

9

Van Zandt

2

Road

Potter

3

4

Miles

0 1 2

END

5

No Bridge

Strand Road

Clipper

6

Standard

7

9

8

JONES CREEK

Acme

River View Park

9

HUTCHINSON CREEK

10

SOUTH FORK

To Wickersham

11

Saxon

12

SAXON CREEK

Saxon Road

START

13

SKOOKUM CREEK

NOOKSACK RIVER

at higher, swifter water levels. In late summer the biggest problem is low water.

The river flows over riffles, forming pools and chutes as it meanders its way slowly, occasionally swiftly, northwestward for the first 4.5 miles to the Highway 9 bridge just north of Acme. River View Park has recently been developed on the left bank of the river just upstream from the bridge (this could easily become a river access point). The Twin Sisters peep over the eastern ridge a time or two in the next few miles.

Agricultural activities are more noticeable below Acme, but there is still plenty of forested riverbank, and the river continues to offer challenges in tight squeezes and a few sharp corners as timber debris litters the river. There is no bridge across the South Fork at Strand Road, as some maps indicate, but the access on river right at the west end of Strand Road is the best on the river.

Meandering through a couple of broad bends, the river slows perceptively in the next few miles, forming more pools and becoming more open, and more obviously agricultural. Downstream from the Potter Road bridge, a poor take-out, the railroad tracks approach the river as it continues to bend broadly and become more woodsy again until it reaches its confluence with the main Nooksack.

The South Fork is a mellow river on a warm sunny day. Boaters might expect to see ospreys, killdeer, kingfishers, spotted sandpipers, violet-green swallows and beaver sign. There are plenty of gravel bars and sandy beaches at midsummer low water levels. At high water levels it might not be as safe a run, and under overcast skies, not as delightful.

5 SKAGIT RIVER MOUTH

Location: south of Mount Vernon
Distance: 3 to 17 miles
River Time: 2 to 5 hours, depending on tides
Maps: Utsalady, Conway (7.5'); NOAA Chart 18423
Best Season: all year, especially winter
Hazards: strong tides and currents, fog
Shuttle: none needed or practical, paved roads for alternate accesses
Rating: B, T

Overview. The mouth of the Skagit River is bifurcated into a North Fork (actually more of a west fork) and a South Fork. Either branch can be run, but the South Fork is more accessible. It also offers better access to the Skagit Flats, where numerous migratory birds winter, including tens of thousands of snow geese. Bald eagles, trumpeter and whistling swans, and numerous ducks and geese are common winter visitors. Year-round residents include great blue herons and great horned owls, as well as shorebirds and bay ducks. The tidal flats also offer interesting marine life.

Access. The best access to the lower South Fork is from the Skagit Wildlife Recreation Area on southern Fir Island southwest of Conway off Mann Road. A boat ramp near a major parking area offers direct access to Freshwater Slough, the most direct route to the Skagit Flats.

There is also public access at Conway on the South Fork before it splits into several sloughs and on the right bank of the river just above the branching of the main forks southwest of Mount Vernon. It is also possible to launch at Edgewater Park in Mount Vernon, from the west (right) bank at RM 11.2, and from a public fishing access just above the river's split around Fir Island at RM 8.5.

There is commercial access at Blake's Marina on the south side of the North Fork at RM 2.5 off Rawlins Road and public access on the south side of the North Fork at RM 4.2 off Moore Road.

Driving Directions. Take the Conway exit (Exit 221) off I-5 and head west through Conway and across the Skagit River Bridge on Fir Island Road. Turn left almost immediately onto Mann Road, which follows the Skagit Dike south, then west to the Skagit Wildlife Recreation Area. The parking area is left of the headquarters area, and the boat ramp lies beyond (over the dike from) the parking area.

An alternate approach is to continue west on Fir Island Road to the other end of Mann Road, which T's in from the left about 2 miles west of the Skagit River Bridge. Follow the signs to the Skagit Wildlife Recreation Area.

Description. At the Skagit Wildlife Recreation Area launch site, the river is deep and swift; a glacial green much of the year, the water is cold and surprisingly clear. It is a salmon and steelhead river and gets heavy fishing pressure, but when the fishing season is closed and the migratory birds are on the Skagit Flats, it is a boater's paradise, even in midwinter.

Paddlers should check weather reports carefully; winter storms can seriously impact Skagit Bay, the saltwater body embracing the flats.

The lower river is well wooded for the first mile or so; saltwater intrusion seems not to adversely affect the alders and cottonwoods that, with a few conifers and assorted shrubbery, form most of the riverside vegetation. Great horned owls congregate in the taller trees along the river even during daylight hours; paddlers may see as many as a dozen owls in the first mile of downriver paddling.

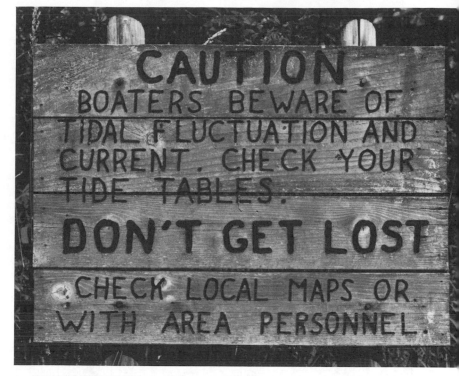

Warning signs near tidal areas should be heeded.

As paddlers near the mouth of Freshwater Slough, the tall trees fade away and the highest vegetation may be the roots of stumps lying about on the flats—as often as not they serve as perches for bald eagles or great blue herons. Tall grasses also replace the tall trees for a few hundred yards, then even the grasses give way to pickleweed and other salt-tolerant species.

The pull of the tide accelerates the flow of the river current, which may move at several miles an hour. This flow enhances the downriver movement of paddle craft but, conversely, is extremely difficult to paddle against. It may be wise to carry a pole, for the bottom is shallow and sandy or gravelly in many places, offering good purchase for poling against the current, should that become necessary. It is better to check the tide charts first.

Once out on the flats, paddlers will see the thousands of snow geese they have been hearing for many minutes. The myriad birds may fly en masse, then settle down to a new feeding area, all the while making a deafening cacophony. The water may move swiftly out from under the craft. Paddlers should remain aware of the flow, lest they become stranded on the Flats. There are numerous tiny channels flowing in dendritic patterns, draining the mud flats. Spending several hours stuck in the mud can be decidedly unpleasant, especially in midwinter.

There is also the possibility of becoming lost in the fog. A compass should be standard equipment for any saltwater venture by canoe. (On one trip to the Skagit Flats, paddlers were fog-bound for more than an hour. They kept their direction by compass and by the flow of water beneath the canoe. When the fog finally lifted, they were right where they'd planned to be.)

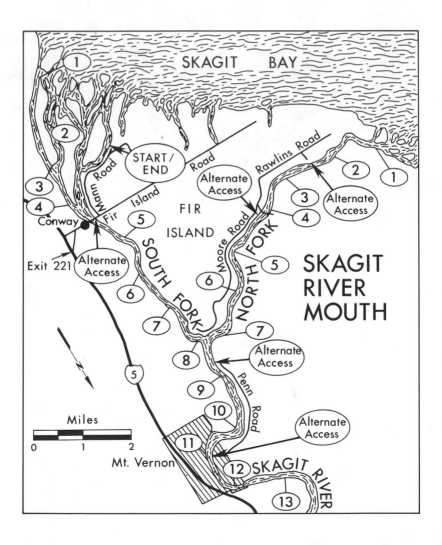

The numerous channels and branches of the Skagit Flats lend themselves to confusion. Be sure to watch the route, selecting certain stumps and promontories as guideposts. It is easy to get lost on the flats. For a first trip, it may be best to join an established group that includes people who have been out before.

When the tide turns, it takes a while for the current to begin to flow upstream with any force, but it will do so eventually, taking the paddlers back to where they started—if they selected the right route. When the river is high, the upstream current created by the tide may not be as strong as desired, but given time and paddle power, the craft will make it back.

To make a 17-mile loop around Fir Island requires reading tides carefully. For instance, paddlers could paddle northwest across the face of the flats, find a channel leading into the North Fork and follow the North Fork upstream some 7.3 miles to its confluence with the South Fork, thence travel down the South Fork to the right-hand channel around the east side of the island just below the bridge at Conway, then pass 1.5 miles farther downstream to the put-in—all with careful consideration of the tides.

6 SAUK RIVER: County Park to Skagit

Location: south and west of Rockport
Distance: 11 to 12 miles
River Time: 2 to 3 hours
Maps: Rockport, Finney Peak (7.5'), Lake Shannon (15')
Best Season: all year, except at flood stage
Hazards: sweepers, logjams, cold and fast water, big river
Shuttle: 10 miles west side, 12 miles via Rockport, paved roads
Rating: C–

Overview. The Lower Sauk as it flows into the Skagit is part of the Skagit River Bald Eagle Natural Area. It is well wooded but provides views of several spectacular peaks. Enhanced by a slough system that can be explored at higher water levels, it is a good place for eagle-watching in the winter. Fishing can be excellent at the mouth of the Sauk, where it joins the Skagit, for steelhead, salmon and sea-run cutthroat trout. This short segment of the lower Sauk, coupled with the Skagit immediately below Rockport, is a seldom-paddled stretch that offers a variety of river experiences.

Access. The best access to this stretch of river is about 5.5 miles south of Rockport. Since the Sauk meets the Skagit less than half a

Sauk River paddlers explore the shoreline.

mile below Rockport, it is also possible to access this stretch from Howard Miller Steelhead Park in Rockport. A take-out can be reached from either Highway 20, 5 miles west of Rockport, or from the Concrete-Sauk Valley Road.

Driving Directions. To reach this portion of the Skagit and its tributary, the lower Sauk, head north on I-5 to Burlington, then take the North Cascade Highway (Highway 20) east to Concrete. Two accesses on opposite sides of the river a few miles upstream from Concrete offer take-out possibilities.

From Concrete, head east on Highway 20 about 4 miles to a public fishing access on river right (south of the highway) at RM 62, where a shuttle vehicle can be left (although there is limited parking). Paddlers can also drive all the way to Rockport (9 miles) to take out at Howard Miller Steelhead Park, but that will mean paddling upstream

SAUK RIVER
(County Park to Skagit)

71

from the mouth of the Sauk against a stiff Skagit current. For a take-out on the left bank, head south out of Concrete on the Sauk Valley Road across the Skagit River toward Darrington, turning left to a Public Fishing Access about 5 miles southeast of town at RM 62.

To reach the put-in from that location, return to the Sauk Valley Road and turn left toward Darrington. Upon reaching the Sauk River County Park, turn left into the main entrance and find a spot nearest the river for a rough carry-to-the-river launch (the huge sandbar that used to offer excellent access to the river was washed away during a flood in the early 1980s).

To reach the put-in from the Highway 20 take-out or from Howard Miller Steelhead Park in Rockport, take Highway 530 south from Rockport (see Map #7). Turn right at the fork about 6 miles south of Rockport, cross the Sauk River, and head northwest on the Concrete-Sauk Valley Road. In roughly half a mile, turn right into the park and scout out a river access from the campground.

Description. The Sauk is a mellow river in this stretch, isolated from the roads and surrounded by tall timber. It is fast-flowing and may be decorated with sweepers and logjams as it nears the Skagit, depending on the debris left by the last high water. The views of nearby Sauk Mountain (5416 feet) to the north and distant Mount Baker (10,775 feet) to the northwest are well worth the trip.

The left bank is relatively low, rising to cut-over mountain land in the Mount Baker-Snoqualmie National Forest. The right bank, also Mount Baker-Snoqualmie National Forest land, is initially steep—except where Hilt Creek comes in at RM 3.3—as the Sauk approaches its delta by breaking through a kind of portal between opposing ridges into the Skagit floodplain. The lower 3 miles of the Sauk is low-lying and marshy.

McLeod Slough branches off to the left, taking 2.2 miles to reach the Skagit at Sauk RM 0.9. The main channel reaches the Skagit at Skagit RM 67.3; McLeod Slough, at Skagit RM 65.9. The delta area changes from year to year as flood waters alter its configuration, but at high water levels it offers some interesting exploration possibilities. The entire mouth, including McLeod Slough, is part of the Skagit River Bald Eagle Natural Area and includes a section of land owned by The Nature Conservancy.

The Skagit itself is a stately river, fast, deep and powerful, the primary reason for the C- rating of this segment (otherwise it would be simply B).There is a large island just below RM 65.9 where McLeod Slough enters the Skagit. It is easier to run on the left if reached from the Slough, but it can normally be run on either side. Between the lower end of the island (RM 65) and the take-out there are several more small islands. The lower ones, between RM 63.5 and the take-out, are usually run on the right, following the main flow.

Kayakers enjoy the mild rapids of the Sauk River.

7 SAUK RIVER: Darrington to Sauk County Park

Location: Darrington north
Distance: 15 miles
River Time: 3 hours
Maps: Darrington, Rockport (7.5')
Best Season: all year, but avoid high water
Hazards: rapids, sweepers, logjams, cold water
Shuttle: 16 miles, Highway 530 most of the way
Rating: C–

Overview. This segment of the Sauk River, part of the National Wild and Scenic Rivers System, offers fine views of the North Cascades, especially the peaks around Darrington. A challenging run for canoeists, it has several mild rapids and some interesting chutes, especially at low water. The current is swift, the water clear much of the year, but it turns milky with glacial flour from midsummer through early fall. Highway 530, which approximately parallels the river, is largely unobtrusive and handy in case of trouble on the river.

Access. There are numerous accesses for this segment of the Sauk, from the put-in by the only bridge across the Sauk in Darrington to the take-out at the Sauk County Park. With Highway 530 following the entire course of the Sauk in this segment, first on the west bank, then on the east, several points suggest themselves as possible put-in or take-out points, including the popular access across from the mouth of the Suiattle and another at the bridge that carries Highway 530 across the Sauk.

Driving Directions. The standard take-out for the run is at the Sauk County Park on the Concrete-Sauk Valley Road west of the Sauk roughly 6 miles south of Rockport. If traveling the North Cascade Highway (Highway 20) to Rockport, head south on Highway 530 toward Darrington. At the fork 6 miles south of town, turn right, cross the Sauk onto the Concrete-Sauk Valley Road, then turn right into the park's main entrance in about half a mile. Leave a shuttle vehicle near the river.

If coming through Darrington, head north on Highway 530 toward Rockport. After crossing the Sauk (to the east bank), Highway 530 turns left (north). After 4 miles, the road forks; Highway 530 continues north to Rockport, and the Concrete-Sauk Valley Road turns off to the left, crosses the Sauk, and passes the Sauk County Park.Turn right into the park and leave a shuttle vehicle.

To reach the put-in, drive to Darrington on Highway 530. North of town turn east onto the road (Crawford Loop Road) immediately south of the town's major lumber mill, and travel toward the bridge over the Sauk. Just before reaching the bridge, turn left onto a paved road between the lumber mill and the bridge that offers access to the left bank of the Sauk beneath the bridge. This is a common take-out for whitewater trips on the upper Sauk and the put-in for this segment.

For any of the alternate take-outs, drive back to Highway 530 and turn right, heading north. Six miles north of Darrington there is an access between Highway 530 and the river, opposite the mouth of the Suiattle, a possible take-out for an 8-mile run. A mile beyond this point the road makes a right-angle turn and crosses the Sauk. Just beyond the bridge on the right shoulder of the road is another access for a take-out on river right just upstream from the bridge.

Description. From the put-in by the lumber mill on the north edge of Darrington, the river meanders northeast for 5 miles, dividing around small gravel islands where logjams may pile up, flowing strongly against cut banks where sweepers may overhang, mumbling over shallow bars where stumps and rocks may offer obstacles. Don't forget to look back upstream for the views of Whitehorse Mountain.

The right bank is low, offering views of peaks in the North Cascades and of the massive clear-cuts on Huckleberry Mountain in the Mount Baker-Snoqualmie National Forest, geometric patterns that follow survey lines. Glacier Peak Wilderness lies just beyond, and the wilderness can be seen from the river, beyond those ugly clear-cuts.

SAUK RIVER
(Darrington to County Park)

To Rockport

Concrete-Sauk Valley Road

6

County Park

END

7

8

9

10

11

12

Alternate Access

13

Alternate Access

SUIATTLE RIVER

14

530

15

PRAIRIE CREEK

16

GRAVEL CREEK

17

18

Crawford Loop Road

20

19

To Arlington

21

530

START

Darrington

SAUK RIVER

Miles

0   1   2

N

At RM 16 the Sauk turns north, as Gravel Creek and then Prairie Creek enter from the right. The Sauk still weaves its way among gravel bars, against cut banks and through timber debris. The views to the east improve as the ridge between the Sauk and the Suiattle descends; and at RM 13 the Suiattle joins the Sauk.

A mile below the mouth of the Suiattle, the river flows under the Highway 530 bridge, then continues almost due north, still swinging from side to side through its floodplain. At RM 9.6, where there is a small rapid that at low water offers several chutes, the Sauk brushes the road (indeed, it washed out part of Highway 530 at this point in the early 1980s) and parallels it closely to the bridge at RM 7, which carries the Concrete-Sauk Valley Road across the Sauk.

There are some large boulders in the river here, creating irregular currents, and there is a small riffle just below the bridge as the river turns left and approaches the take-out on river left at the Sauk County Park. Sauk Mountain looms downstream, as the peaks upstream diminish with distance and the bends of the river.

8 SKAGIT RIVER: Marblemount to Rockport

Location: along North Cascades Highway (Highway 20)
Distance: 10 miles
River Time: 2 to 3 hours
Maps: Marblemount (15'), Rockport (7.5')
Best Season: all year, eagle-watching in winter
Hazards: sweepers, logjams, cold and swift water
Shuttle: 9 miles, Highway 20 most of the way
Rating: B

Overview. This segment is the famous eagle run, the stretch of river that has the greatest concentration of wintering bald eagles from November through February (as many as 173 eagles have been seen on a single 2-hour trip). Much of the shoreline is in private ownership, but much of the best eagle habitat is owned and protected by The Nature Conservancy in the Skagit River Bald Eagle Natural Area. Boaters are requested to launch between 10 A.M. and noon, to float quietly, minimizing movement and noise, and to refrain from stopping between Marblemount and Rockport.

Access. The most popular put-in is beneath the bridge over the Skagit, on Cascade Road in Marblemount. The usual take-out is at

Bald eagles on the winter Skagit.

Howard Miller Steelhead Park in Rockport, where there is a well-used boat ramp.

Driving Directions. To reach the take-out, drive to Rockport. Immediately north of the Highway 530 bridge across the Skagit, turn into Howard Miller Steelhead Park and drive west a hundred yards; the boat ramp is on the left of the road, on river right.

To reach the put-in, take Highway 20 to Marblemount, but where the highway turns left in Marblemount, go straight across the bridge eastward (or, if coming from the northeast, turn left onto Cascade Road at the right-angle turn in Marblemount). Immediately east of the bridge, turn left onto a road that doubles back on the north side of Cascade Road and leads to the river access beneath the bridge on river left.

Description. From the popular launch site under the bridge at the east edge of Marblemount, the river flows gently south past the mouth of the Cascade River, another element of the National Wild and Scenic Rivers System, as is this part of the Skagit. It turns west (forming a deep pool next to a modest cliff), then north, then west again in a big bend through Marblemount. It flows past the back yards of residences, through Studebaker Hole (named for the old car body once used as rip-rap that has lodged on the left bank), and over a little riffle as the river narrows to the left.

The road embraces the river for a mile, then drops away as the river flows beneath some high-power cables carrying electricity to Seattle

SKAGIT RIVER

(Copper Creek to Marblemount and Marblemount to Rockport)

from the dams upstream. Beaver cuts appear near the power line crossing, as tiny Corkindale Creek flows in from the right (north). The left bank, privately owned, is lined with cabins and weekend homes. Rocky Creek comes in from the right at a point where many commercial river trips stop for lunch.

Immediately downstream, the major eagle concentration begins just as the river divides around an island. The usual route is to the right, but at higher water levels, the left-hand channel is possible, though it may have more logjams and sweepers than the main-flow right-hand route. In the next few miles the river splits and meanders, providing the eagles with daytime roosts and gravel bars for feeding on the spawned-out salmon that litter the shore in late fall and early winter.

The river approaches the road a time or two, then gathers itself together for a long straight run (nearly 2 miles) below the mouth of Illabot Slough/Creek. It splits again, turns south through some choppy waves, then curves west once more before splitting into several channels (generally stay right) just above Rockport. Just after the river flows beneath the bridge (Highway 530), there is a busy boat ramp on the right bank at Howard Miller Steelhead Park, the take-out.

In the spring, summer and fall this stretch makes a pleasant paddle with a few mild rapids, but from early November through mid-March this stretch is the bald eagles' wintering grounds. Boating is permitted but paddlers are requested to restrict their river use to specific hours (10 A.M. until noon) and to make no stops along the route.

9 SKAGIT RIVER: Copper Creek to Marblemount

Location: along North Cascades Highway (Highway 20), northeast of Marblemount
Distance: 6 miles
River Time: 2 hours
Map: Marblemount (15')
Best Season: autumn, but nice all year
Hazards: sweepers, logjams, minor rapids (chutes)
Shuttle: 7 miles, mostly along Highway 20
Rating: B–

Overview. The Skagit River above Marblemount is clear and cold with a greenish tint that gives it an almost pristine quality despite its reservoir-release origin. During autumn salmon migrations, especially in odd-numbered years (1989, 1991) this stretch of river is an

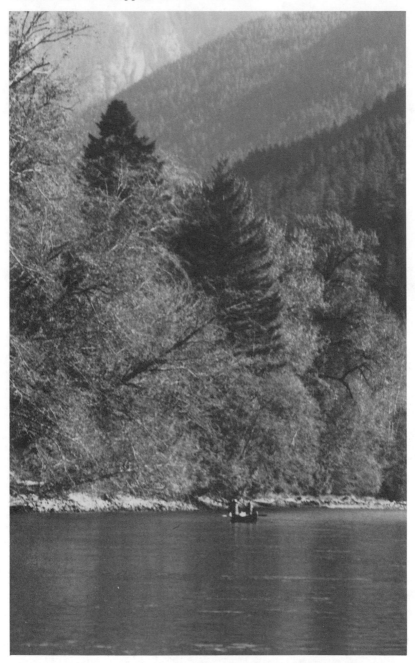

The Skagit River, with North Cascades National Park in the background.

impressive spawning stream. The streamside vegetation offers some of the finest autumn color in the North Cascades, and the fishing can be excellent, especially for sea-run cutthroat trout. It is a short stretch, with Highway 20 along much of the route, but its roadless portions offer quiet solitude.

Access. Access is from a launch site opposite the mouth of Copper Creek, within the Ross Lake National Recreation Area, and at the popular boating access beneath the bridge in Marblemount. Other accesses are possible along Highway 20 between the put-in and the take-out.

Driving Directions. To reach the take-out, drive east on Highway 20. Where the highway turns left in Marblemount, simply drive straight ahead onto the Cascade River Road and across the Skagit River bridge (the bridge will be visible before Highway 20 makes its turn to the north). Immediately beyond the bridge, turn left onto a dirt road that doubles back north of the bridge and leads to the river-bank beneath the bridge on river left. This is the take-out for this run and the put-in for run #8 to Rockport.

To reach the put-in, recross the bridge and turn right to head north up the North Cascades Highway (Highway 20) toward Newhalem. After crossing the bridge over Bacon Creek, which flows into the Skagit within sight of the bridge, you will enter the Ross Lake National Recreation Area. Within half a mile, between mileposts 111 and 112, on a slight bend in the road to the left, there is a dirt road on the right. Turn right on that road and follow it to the river and the put-in.

Description. The first mile of river is as peaceful and pristine as any, a favorite salmon spawning stretch where vine maple and old man's beard offer colorful contrasts in the fall. At the end of the first mile, Bacon Creek comes in on the right, an important salmon spawning tributary where dozens of fish may be seen working their way upstream.

Below the Bacon Creek delta, the river swings to the left through a series of chutes, the only rapid on this stretch. The river broadens and shallows below this point, providing excellent spawning beds for the salmon, which can be seen in the clear water during the fall. An old cabin moulders in the rain forest on the left bank.

The road follows the river rather closely for the remainder of this short trip, but the wooded left bank suggests a deeper wilderness than exists, and the bucolic setting conveys a peacefulness well worth experiencing. Even though the cozy little homes along the right bank represent development, it is both gentle and historical, for the most part, fitting into the natural world of the Skagit.

10 *STILLAGUAMISH RIVER*

Location: Arlington to Hat Slough
Distance: 16 miles
River Time: 4 to 5 hours, less at high water
Maps: Arlington, Stanwood (7.5'); NOAA Charts: 18400, 18423
Best Season: early spring through autumn, all year
Hazards: logjams, sweepers, low dam, mild rapids
Shuttle: 14 miles on paved roads
Rating: B–

Overview. The Stillaguamish, meaning "river people," is a favorite steelhead river that flows through farmlands between Arlington and Port Susan. The Stilly—as it is known in local jargon—is a mellow river, marred in a few places by thoughtless human activity and by barnyard smells, but nevertheless full of wildlife (deer, beaver, plenty of birdlife). There is a low dam to portage within view of the I-5 bridges, and the lower few miles are tidal. This rural river is picturesque and pleasant, its bottom sandy and its shoreline well vegetated and marked by a few high bluffs.

Access. Access is available at two parks in Arlington: (1) the park to the east of Highway 530 just beyond the bridge across the South Fork northeast of Arlington, which provides access to the South Fork 0.5 mile above the confluence; and (2) Haller Park on Highway 9 immediately below the confluence of the two forks of the Stilly, just north of downtown Arlington.

The logical take-out is south of Stanwood at a newly developed (1987) access on Hat Slough, the south mouth of the Stilly, just west of Marine Drive.

Driving Directions. To reach the take-out, use the Highway 530 exit (Exit 208) from I-5 and head west toward Silvana through low-lying farming country; pass through Silvana; just after crossing the bridge over the North Branch, about 4 miles from I-5, turn left onto Norman Road and follow it west. Norman Road becomes 238th Street NW. There is a low-overhead railroad underpass (10 feet 5 inches) that may be a hazard to canoes on cartop carriers on vans, in which case use the alternative approach mentioned below.

At Marine Drive, turn left, then right almost immediately (before the bridge across the Stilly, or Hat Slough as this south mouth is called) onto the road that parallels Hat Slough on the north bank (236th Street NW). The river access (take-out) is left of the road at a boat ramp. There is limited parking here.

An alternate route for reaching the take-out is to leave I-5 at the Stanwood exit (Highway 532, Exit 212) and head west toward Stanwood, then take Marine Drive south to 236th Street NW, and turn right to the take-out.

To reach the put-in at Arlington, retrace the route to I-5, heading east on Highway 530 to Arlington, where there are two possible launch sites: (1) turn left onto Highway 9 and head north only a couple of blocks to Haller Park on the left. This access is on the left bank of the Stilly, below the Highway 9 bridge and less than 0.1 mile below the confluence of the forks that create the Stillaguamish; (2) go through town following Highway 530 toward Darrington. Just after crossing the bridge over the South Fork at the northeast edge of town, turn right into a small riverside park that offers access to the right bank of the lower 0.5 mile of the South Fork.

Description. From the South Fork access, the river flows placidly past a bluff on the left on which part of Arlington is built. A few riffles and logjams and then the South Fork joins the North Fork in a swirl of currents that can be tricky. Less experienced paddlers may want to put in at Haller Park immediately below this juncture.

Riverside vegetation along the Stillaguamish.

From Haller Park (RM 17.8) the river flows slowly over a sandy bottom, past sand and gravel bars and a few riffles, the banks lined with stately cottonwoods. There are rocks and logs in the water (which is clear most of the year), a few tight chutes at low water, a few sweepers at high water. Soon the left bank is encased in concrete. The noise of machinery and barnyard smells invade the river from adjacent gravel pits and dairies, but beaver signs attest to the presence of those primarily nocturnal rodents, and birds are abundant (robins, black-headed grosbeaks, killdeer, mallards, spotted sandpipers, linnets).

It is a broad, slow river lined with grasses, maples, Douglas fir, western red cedar, hemlock and cottonwoods. At RM 12—just above the double I-5 bridge—Bed Rock Rapid offers a mild challenge, as do occasional logjams that create tight corners. But the biggest challenge lies just 0.25 mile below I-5: a low diversion dam that may best be portaged or lined. At certain water levels it creates what could be a dangerous hydraulic keeper (reversal current) across the face of the dam. It can be scouted from Gulhagen Road off Highway 530.

The river begins to swing broadly through its floodplain under bridges (railroad and highway), past a trailer park with a gravel beach (river right) opposite a steep bluff (river left). The river marge is well vegetated with willow, which provides habitat for deer and numerous birds, including the varied thrush and kingfisher. The lower 3 miles are under tidal influence, and marine species begin to appear; at low tide there are mud flats on each shore. The take-out is on river right at RM 1.8.

11 STILLAGUAMISH RIVER: North Fork

Location: between Arlington and Darrington
Distance: 8 miles
River Time: 2 hours
Map: Oso (15')
Best Season: all year, may be too low August-September
Hazards: sweepers, logjams, Class II rapids
Shuttle: 6.4 miles on Highway 530, ideal for bicycle
Rating: B+

Overview. The North Fork of the Stillaguamish is a lovely stream that flows westward from near the North Cascades timber town of Darrington to Arlington through a bucolic valley of old farms and

North Cascade peaks guard the North Fork of the Stillaguamish.

small homesteads. It offers grand views of the Cascade peaks and, in the winter, a bit of eagle watching. Its valley is rural enough to foster good wildlife, and its climate mild enough to be runnable any time there is enough water. There can also be too much water, however, for the river floods with heavy winter rains, and boaters don't want to be on it at flood stage.

Access. Since the road (Highway 530) follows the river and crosses it twice, there are several potential access points. The most appropriate are the take-out for this segment at the Washington Wildlife Department access off Monty Road at Cicero near the Highway 530 bridge 9 miles east of Arlington and the put-in at the Evergreen Fly Fishing Club access between the railroad tracks and the river on Whitman Road (251st Avenue, NE) at Halterman.

Driving Directions. Leave a shuttle vehicle—a bicycle will do nicely—at the Department of Wildlife access off Monty Road, 8.7 miles east of the junction of Highway 9 and Highway 530 in Arlington. This is just west of the aesthetically pleasing bridge across the North Fork and north of the highway. The best boating take-out is under the railroad bridge immediately south of the highway (across from the public access area; there is an eddy there, with a nasty logjam just below it). This take-out over the rip-rapped bank is easier than the often-muddy trail through the brambles below the logjam.

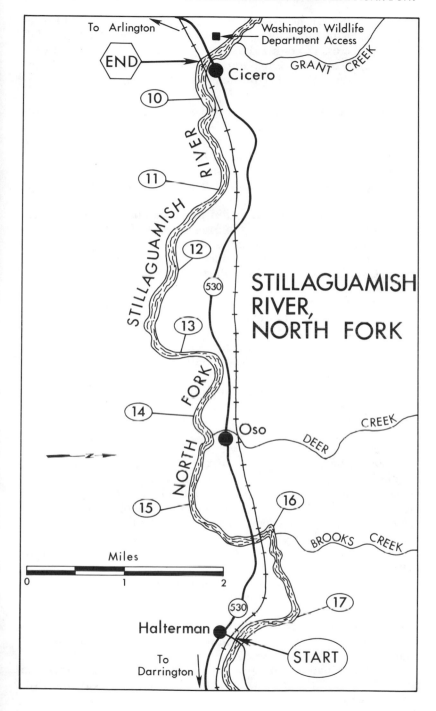

To Arlington

Washington Wildlife
Department Access

END

Cicero

GRANT CREEK

10

STILLAGUAMISH RIVER

11

12

530

STILLAGUAMISH
RIVER,
NORTH FORK

13

NORTH FORK

14

Oso

DEER CREEK

15

16

BROOKS CREEK

Miles

0   1   2

530

17

Halterman

START

To
Darrington

To reach the put-in, drive east on Highway 530 through Oso for about 7 miles to the Whitman Road (251st Avenue, NE), turn left (north) and cross the railroad tracks. The access, which lies between the tracks and the river, is maintained and used regularly by the Evergreen Fly Fishing Club. The put-in is on river left under the bridge.

Description. The North Fork is rocky in its first few hundred yards with a riffle or two before it reaches a dogleg to the left at the most severe rapid on this segment. Here it runs to the very edge of the Mount Baker-Snoqualmie National Forest (which borders the river for the next mile) before it swings south under the railroad and highway bridges to flow past the foot of Wheeler Mountain on the south side of the floodplain.

There are a number of vacation homes along the south-bound stretch of the North Fork. It soon bends west in a broad sweeping curve to the right, leaving a wide gravel bar on the right where steelhead fishermen gather to try their luck. Take care in boating past fishermen. Courteous boaters avoid interfering with the activities of other river users.

The river gets progressively easier downstream, and the views upstream progressively improve. Whitehorse Mountain can be seen from a number of stretches below Oso, which can be recognized by the bridge that crosses the river just south of town (no access here) and by the entry of Deer Creek, which flows into the North Fork just southwest of Oso.

Barnyard smells mingle with the odor of fresh-cut cedar from the small mill near Oso, and you can even smell the raspberries in adjacent fields in midsummer. Spotted sandpipers, kingfishers, great blue herons, robins, and yellow warblers add color and variety to the trip, and old barns offer picturesque views.

There are vacation homes and year-round residences along the river, as well as private picnic areas and trailers. Riverside vegetation includes blackberries, red osier dogwood, tall grasses, and the usual deciduous trees: tall cottonwoods, alders and maples. The sound of farm machinery and logging trucks intrudes into the river corridor at times, but generally this is a quiet segment with distant views of Cascade peaks and forested hillsides, marred here and there by the inevitable clear-cuts.

The take-out under the bridge is steep, a rough haul over rip-rap boulders, but the logjam a hundred yards downstream can be hairy in high water, and its location makes it difficult to land on the left bank, where the access trail is. The eddy under the bridge offers quiet water for a take-out, and there is a small parking area, better used to load boats than for parking, between the highway and the railroad.

The Monty Road access may also be used for launching a run on the North Fork to Arlington, where the two main forks of the Stillaguamish converge just a hundred yards above the Haller Park access in Arlington. This stretch of river goes through a short but pleasant canyon but adds 9.5 miles to the trip. Of course, it can be run as an entirely separate trip another day.

12 STILLAGUAMISH RIVER: South Fork

Location: between Granite Falls and Arlington
Distance: 11 miles
River Time: 4 hours
Maps: Granite Falls (15'), Lake Stevens, Arlington (7.5')
Best Season: early spring through summer, all year
Hazards: sweepers, logjams, Class II rapids
Shuttle: 8.3 miles, mostly on paved road
Rating: B

Overview. The South Fork of the Stillaguamish is another favorite steelhead stream flowing through a rural area. Its background bluffs give it the appearance of an Ozark river, but its vegetation is strictly Pacific Northwestern. A broad but lively river, most of its real action comes within the first few miles of the segment. Alternating pools and riffles, the river is rocky, a good poling river challenging enough in its moderate rapids to provide practice in basic canoeing techniques.This segment is a favorite trip for the Paddle Trails Canoe Club.

Access. Three major access points on the South Fork between Granite Falls and Arlington offer opportunities for running several different segments: (1) beneath the bridge across the South Fork just north of Granite Falls, (2) beneath the suspension footbridge at Jordan about 7 river miles below access 1, and (3) at River Meadows County Park another 4 river miles downstream. A fourth access is at the park at the northeast edge of Arlington that may be used as a launch site for Trip #10.

Driving Directions. To reach either of the parks in Arlington, which might serve as take-outs for longer runs, follow the directions in Trip #10.

To reach River Meadows County Park, take the Highway 530 exit off I-5 (Exit 208), and head east to Arlington. Go through town as though following Highway 530 to Darrington, and turn right onto Arlington Heights Road about a mile beyond the bridge across the

Lunch stop on the South Fork of the Stillaguamish.

South Fork. In about a mile, turn right again, onto Jordan Road, and follow it southeast toward Jordan. In about 3 miles turn right into River Meadows County Park, drive down the hill to the parking area, which is within an easy carry of the riverbank. Spot a shuttle vehicle here.

Drive back to Jordan Road (also known as the Granite Falls-Arlington Road), turn right and drive the 8.3 miles to the bridge across the South Fork, just north of Granite Falls. The put-in is on the left (that is, the upstream side of the bridge) just before the bridge.

On the drive from River Meadows County Park to the put-in, you will pass through Jordan, a tiny community with a small parking area (six cars at most) on the south side of the road, accessed by way of a suspension footbridge to a small park with a broad beach on river left under the bridge. It makes a strenuous carry, but it is possible to launch or take out at this point, dividing this run into a 7- and a 4-mile run, above and below this point.

To go more directly to the launch site, take Highway 92 off Highway 9 north of Lake Stevens and travel northeast toward Granite Falls. Just before reaching the city streets, turn left onto Jordan Road, which jogs around a bit but heads generally north to cross the South Fork. Immediately past the bridge, turn right into a public fishing access area, which is the launch site.

STILLAGUAMISH RIVER: South Fork

Description. From the launch site beneath the bridge, the river is clear, rocky and rapid. Ideal for poling, the river is shallow with a gravel or rocky bottom. There are also lovely deep green pools, followed by a couple of 3- to 4-foot drops, good Class II rapids. Fully half the action of this segment occurs in the first mile.

There are a couple of small islands on the second turn with a third drop (rapid) just below them; then the river mellows out and the wildlife appears (or rather, you have time to notice it). Mergansers, ravens, spotted sandpipers, and great blue herons can be sighted. Houses appear on the left bank, a series of miniature waterfalls, then a ledge of fossil shells—all on the left. It is a pool-and-drop river with sandy beaches often opposite shallow cliffs.

The banks are lined with vine maple, western red cedar, Douglas fir, hemlock, alder, and in season, bright yellow monkey flowers. The bird life includes bald eagles, several species of swallows, more ducks. The suspension bridge at Jordan, throwing its shadow into the deep pools at the edge of the park beach, marks 7 miles from the launch.

Below Jordan the river gets slower, broader, shallower, and more

Eroded bluffs along the South Fork of the Stillaguamish.

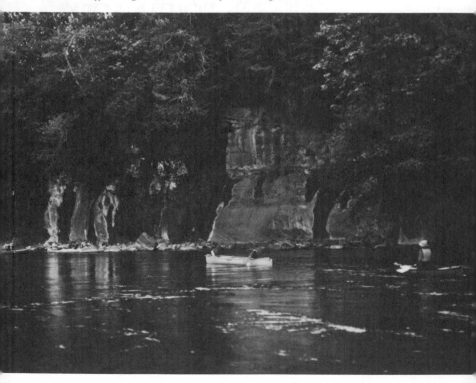

agricultural in the final 4 miles of this segment, a trend that continues all the way to Arlington. Many paddlers take out at River Meadows County Park because it is convenient—though a long carry in late summer when the gravel bar widens with low water—and because the river slows below the park. To Arlington from the park is another 4 miles, a good hour's hard paddling in slow water.

13 *SNOHOMISH RIVER SLOUGHS*

Location: north and east of Everett
Distance: from 3 to 23 miles
River Time: 3 miles per hour on average
Maps: Marysville, Everett, Snohomish (7.5'); NOAA Charts: 18423, 18443, 18444
Best Season: all year
Hazards: contrary tides, power boats
Shuttle: none necessary, paved roads for alternate accesses
Rating: A, T

Overview. The Snohomish River Sloughs—Ebey, Steamboat, Union—and the mouth of the Snohomish River itself offer more than 40 miles of paddling potential, a veritable network of waterways in which a paddler could get lost and paddle for days with the tide, moving upstream and down with the ebb and flow. There is industrial development along much of the shoreline, but the area also serves as wonderful waterfowl habitat. The women's Olympic crew team has used the lower river and some of its sloughs for their training, and fishermen, many of them in power boats, make regular use of the slough, as do hunters in waterfowl season.

Access. There is amazingly little public access to the lower Snohomish and its sloughs. The best access is from the Smith Island public boat launch, the newly developed (1988) Langus Riverside Park on the lower main stem of the river, about 3 miles upstream from its mouth in Everett Harbor.

There is public boating access at the waterfront park in Everett, but it involves paddling across the face of Everett Harbor to reach the mouth of the river or any of the sloughs. There is a fee for launching.

Other potential accesses are at Lowell about 7 miles from the mouth (4 miles above the access mentioned above), and about a mile

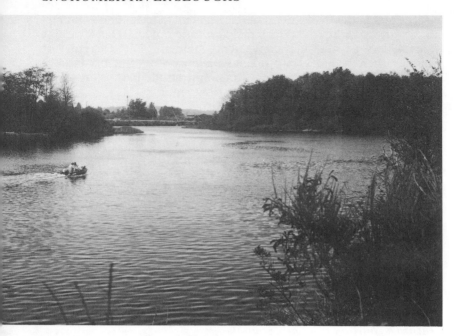

Power boaters ply the lower Snohomish.

upstream from Lowell, off River Road (8 miles from the mouth of the river).

Driving Directions. To reach the access 3 miles from the mouth of the Snohomish River heading south on I-5, take the Highway 529 exit off I-5 (Exit 198), head south off Highway 529, following first Frontage Road, then 24th Street NE (also Ross Avenue) to Smith Island Road, following the signs to Langus Riverside Park (formerly Smith Island Park) developed and maintained by the Everett Parks Department. To reach this access from the south (driving north on I-5) take Exit 195 and turn left on Marine View Drive to Highway 529 heading north, then turn right onto 28th Place, right again onto 35th Avenue to Smith Island Road and turn left, following it to the park and access.

To reach the 10th Street waterfront park in Everett, take I-5 Exit 195 heading north onto Grand Avenue, which becomes East Marine Drive under I-5 as it swings northwest to loop around the north end of the peninsula on which most of north Everett is built. It becomes West Marine Drive as it swings south and the cross street numbers begin to climb. At 10th Street turn right into the waterfront park and boat launch.

SNOHOMISH RIVER SLOUGHS

To reach Lowell, take I-5 south to Exit 192 (the Broadway/Lowell Road) and head south to Lenora Street, turn left and head for the river on what becomes Lowell River Road. At the edge of Lowell, there is a steep, rough access on the left bank of the river bend left of the road. A mile beyond this access (southeast) is a water pipeline crossing and a public access left of Lowell River Road on the left bank of the river—just downstream from Ebey Slough (which branches off the lower Snohomish River just above this access).

Description. From the launch site at the Smith Island Public Boat Launch paddlers may head downstream toward the Everett waterfront to paddle south to the Port of Everett or turn north, to paddle the sloughs. Careful scrutiny of tide charts will make this an easier and more pleasant trip. It is possible to paddle up Steamboat Slough, the first major waterway north of the river mouth, or Ebey Slough, which flows into Possession Sound a mile north of the river mouth. Union Slough splits off of Steamboat Slough about a mile from its mouth.

The waterfront is developed and industrial, a port for some large ocean-going vessels (and it will become more so as the Navy develops its homeport here). To the north there is a storage area for millions of logs, largely at the mouths of the sloughs. Despite the development, this is good wildlife habitat for shorebirds, waterfowl and bald eagles. The farther up the sloughs you paddle, the farther you get from industrial development and the background noise of I-5 traffic, which dominates their lower 2 or 3 miles.

Ebey Slough and Steamboat Slough entwine twice at RM 5.2 and RM 6.4 at high water levels (high tide). Union Slough and Steamboat Slough, having run 4.4 and 6.2 miles respectively, join at RM 4 on the lower Snohomish. Ebey Slough splits off the river at RM 8.1, flowing 12.4 miles to the Sound, a decided long-cut.

Going upriver from the Smith Island Launch Site, again with careful study of tide charts, paddlers pass under the double span of the I-5 bridge, skirt the industrial northeast edge of Everett, meet the take-off point of the twin sloughs, Union and Steamboat, at RM 4, then skirt the ridge carrying I-5 and much of southeast Everett until they reach Lowell. Here the river turns abruptly away from the ridge and heads eastward (remember, you are going upstream).

Ebey Slough, a mile above Lowell, is controlled by floodgates. This barrier can be portaged and—if the tide is right—this slack-water route can be followed to the Sound, using the tide to increase the craft's speed.

It is also possible to paddle downstream on the Snohomish from Cady Park in Snohomish (see Trip #14) to either of the take-outs suggested above; it is a 10-mile run from Cady Park to Riverfront Park, a 3-hour paddle.

The confluence of the Skykomish (left) with the Snoqualmie (right) forms the Snohomish (foreground).

14 *SNOHOMISH RIVER: Confluence to Snohomish*

Location: Snohomish, south of Snohomish
Distance: 8 miles
River Time: 2 to 3 hours
Maps: Snohomish, Maltby (7.5'), Everett (15')
Best Season: all year, especially summer
Hazards: logjams, sweepers, power boaters
Shuttle: 13 miles by main roads
Rating: B–

Overview. The Snohomish River begins where the Snoqualmie and the Skykomish join, roughly 20 miles from its mouth. More than half of its length is under tidal influence, which reaches well above the town of Snohomish. This segment is mellow, a cool, clear green river easy to paddle for its slow current and braided channel full of islands. Its backdrop changes by slow degrees from forested and mildly isolated, through agricultural, to developed. It offers good birding, especially Canada geese and killdeer, and an opportunity to watch skydiving and biplane acrobatics.

Access. There is an excellent take-out for this segment at Cady Park in Snohomish. Three possible put-in points suggest themselves (see also Map #15): (1) the confluence of the Skykomish and Snoqualmie by way of local roads southwest of Monroe beneath Highway 522, (2) the public boat launch on the Skykomish immediately south of Monroe 4 miles upstream from the confluence, (3) the High Bridge public fishing access on the Snoqualmie 2.8 miles upstream from the confluence.

Driving Directions. To reach the take-out at Cady Park in Snohomish, drive to the town of Snohomish using U.S. Highway 2 or Highway 9. From U.S. Highway 2, take the exit east of town, head west on 92nd Street SE, which becomes Second Street in Snohomish, turn left onto Maple Street and follow it to its end at Cady Park. From Highway 9 take the exit west of town (Foster Slough/River Road), head east into town, take the fork to the right, which is First Street, turn right onto Maple Street and follow it to its end (only one block) to Cady Park.

To find the put-in at the confluence, take U.S. Highway 2 east toward Stevens Pass to Highway 522 just west of Monroe. Follow Highway 522 southwest (toward Woodinville and Seattle) to the Snohomish/Monroe Road. After exiting to the right, turn left under the Highway 522 overpass, toward Monroe, and almost immediately turn right onto Tester Road. Tester Road essentially parallels Highway 522 in a southwesterly direction, becoming 162nd, 176th, 159th, then 180th Street as it follows Highway 522 to the bridge across the Snohomish River. Under the bridge there is a rough access to the river a few hundred yards below the confluence. This shuttle is roughly 13 miles.

To find the access south of Monroe (see Map #15), take U.S. Highway 2 east toward Stevens Pass, turning right in Monroe onto Highway 203 and heading south toward Duvall, Carnation and Fall City. Just before reaching the bridge across the Skykomish immediately south of town, turn right onto a dirt road that constitutes a public boating access. This shuttle is roughly 14 miles. This upstream extension of Trip #14 is described in Trip #15.

Reaching the High Bridge access on the Snoqualmie is complicated.

SNOHOMISH
RIVER

(Confluence to Snohomish)

Miles

From Snohomish head south on Highway 9, turning left at Ree's Corner onto Broadway (99th) to Cathcart, where 164th SE coming in from the right eventually becomes Elliott Road (Connely Road on some maps), which winds around approximately paralleling the river and heading upstream. Some 3 miles after Elliott Road passes under Highway 522 at Three Rivers Park (stay left at the fork 1.5 miles beyond), turn left onto High Bridge Road. Just past the bridge, turn left into a public fishing access to launch. This shuttle is roughly 12 miles.

Description. The 4-mile run on the Skykomish from Monroe to the confluence can be tricky at low water when the current flows strongly beneath sweepers in a place or two. The Skykomish meanders from bank to bank with large gravel bars forcing the current back and forth into sweepers (on one river trip a canoe capsized near the left bank about 3 miles below Monroe on this stretch).

The 2.8-mile lower stretch of the Snoqualmie is like a Southern swamp: except for a riffle a few hundred yards above the confluence with the Skykomish, it is slow and sluggish (except at high water) and heavily forested. At the confluence, the two rivers meet then flow around an island. Depending on water levels and the action of the last flood, the island may be in any one of the three rivers that meet here, the Skykomish and Snoqualmie joining to create the Snohomish.

From the confluence of the Skykomish and the Snoqualmie, the Snohomish River passes under the long angular bridge of Highway 522, then flows placidly past forested banks with cottonwoods along the river, Douglas fir, hemlock and western red cedar on the ridges. There are some farm houses and rural residences and, on the left bank, a trailer park. For 3 miles the river flows fairly straight, the channel braiding among islands, then it takes an abrupt turn to the right, the beginning of a huge "S" where the river spreads out. Here there is much timber debris in the river, well anchored in a sandy bottom. Shorts Road provides rough access along the final bend of the "S" at RM 16.3-16.5.

The river continues to split around islands, the water level determining how navigable any channel may be. A private beach offers swimming and sunbathing opportunities at roughly RM 15 as the farmlands begin to become evident. Flocks of Canada geese and coveys of killdeer frequent the gravel bars, and power boats begin to appear. On sunny days you may be able to observe skydivers and biplane acrobatics at the local airport just south of Snohomish (river left).

As paddlers approach the town of Snohomish, they may notice the mouth of the Pilchuck River coming in on the right just after they pass beneath the first of two railroad bridges. The second railroad bridge announces the take-out 0.25 mile downstream on the right bank at Cady Park.

15 SKYKOMISH RIVER:
Monroe to Confluence

Location: southwest of Monroe
Distance: 4 miles
River Time: 1 hour
Maps: Monroe, Maltby (7.5')
Best Season: all year, especially summer
Hazards: logjams, sweepers
Shuttle: 4 miles on paved roads and city streets
Rating: B

Overview. This short segment of the lower Skykomish is a delightful run and can easily be coupled with a run up the Snoqualmie to the

Deer can be seen along many Western Washington rivers.

High Bridge access or a run all the way (8 more miles) to Snohomish. The area through which it flows is agricultural, but unobtrusively so, and full of wildlife. At high water it is a flush down a big river with few obstacles; at low water it requires more maneuvering because a few bends carry most of the flow under some serious sweepers.

Access. The take-out at the confluence is rugged enough to encourage the paddler to consider two other options: (1) the 8-mile run to Cady Park in Snohomish, extending the trip time from an hour to 3 or 4, and (2) an upstream paddle (or pole) of less than 3 miles to the High Bridge access. The confluence take-out is not all that bad, but it changes with each flood and can be a muddy nuisance.

Driving Directions. To reach the take-out at the confluence, take Highway 522 to Monroe. At the southwest edge of Monroe—near the State Reformatory—turn right onto the Snohomish-Monroe Road as if going into Monroe, then turn right again almost immediately onto Tester Road and follow it as it doubles back toward the river.

It first becomes 162nd, then 176th, 159th, and 180th as it parallels Highway 522, but stay with it. It leads to a riverside/roadside parking area beneath the Highway 522 bridge across the Snohomish, which has come into existence a few hundred yards upstream of the confluence of the Skykomish and the Snoqualmie.

To reach the launch site, retrace the route to the road off Highway 522 (West Main Street), turn right and go into downtown Monroe, turn right onto South Lewis Street (also Highway 203) and drive south to the edge of town. Before reaching the bridge, turn right onto a road that offers access to the Skykomish River's right bank below the bridge.

Description. The Sky—shorthand for Skykomish—is broad and deep here, and green most of the year. It soon shallows and, at low water levels, meanders from bank to bank between gravel bars. Farms line the banks, but agricultural activities do not intrude into the river corridor, and the area is full of wildlife (deer, beaver, raccoon,and numerous bird species, including osprey and eagles).

At low water levels the river seems to disappear downriver; then the channel shows itself swinging off to the left where it hugs the bank after running over a shallow bar that pinches the current into a narrow chute. The current swings back to the right for a time, clear and green as it ripples over the shallows, then swings again hard against the left bank under a sturdy sweeper that has upset a number of paddle craft over the years. Inexperienced paddlers may want to portage or line at certain water levels or take a different channel, even if the craft has to be walked through. Islands occur at higher water levels; in selecting routes, it is generally best to follow the stronger current.

Within sight of the confluence there is a rocky promontory on the left bank that makes a nice lunch stop. From the rock, which makes a good diving platform for the deep pool adjacent, the summer sunbathers and swingers of ropes from the bridge can be observed at the take-out beach on the right.

This take-out beach beneath the bridge also serves as a launch for running the Snohomish to the town of Snohomish (see Trip #14) or all the way to Everett. It is also possible to make an upriver run on the lower 3 miles of the Snoqualmie. At the juncture of the two rivers, simply turn left upstream against the current and paddle hard. The only real problem is a riffle less than a mile above the confluence, and it can be walked, lined or poled at midsummer low water levels.

16 SKYKOMISH RIVER: Sultan to Monroe

Location: east of Monroe along U.S. Highway 2
Distance: 9.5 miles
River Time: 2 to 3 hours
Maps: Sultan, Monroe (7.5')
Best Season: all year, especially summer
Hazards: sweepers, narrow chutes at low water levels
Shuttle: 9 miles on paved roads
Rating: B

Overview. The Skykomish between Sultan and Monroe offers excellent steelhead fishing. It sweeps widely within its floodplain, meandering between huge gravel bars, the shoreline protected by giant cottonwoods. As it hugs the south side of its floodplain, it embraces steep hills that leave the river in shadow much of the year, a cold river where steelheaders gather to try their luck. The adjacent agricultural lands through which the river meanders are hardly noticed from the river, so dense is the streamside vegetation in most of this stretch.

Access. The obvious access for the put-in is the small park on the lower Sultan River just west of the town of Sultan. A good take-out lies just south of Monroe on the right bank below the Highway 203 bridge. An alternate access point, heavily used by fishermen, lies about 2 miles upstream from the Highway 203 bridge on Ben Howard Road, which parallels U.S. Highway 2 on the south side of the river.

Driving Directions. To reach the take-out, drive east on U.S. Highway 2 into Monroe, turn right (south) on Highway 203 to the south edge of town. Just before reaching the bridge across the Skykomish, turn right onto a dirt road paralleling the river that offers public fishing access (and boating as well).

The standard launch site lies at the mouth of the Sultan River just west of Sultan. To reach it from the Monroe take-out, head north on Highway 203 through town, turn right onto U.S. Highway 2 and head east to the west edge of Sultan. Just before reaching the bridge across the Sultan River, turn left into the small park. The launch site is beneath the railroad bridge that parallels the highway bridge across the mouth of the Sultan River.

To reach the alternate access on the left bank 2 miles above Monroe, take the Ben Howard Road, which essentially parallels U.S. Highway 2 south of the river. The east end of Ben Howard Road can be reached by taking the bridge across the Sky in downtown Sultan.

To Duvall

25

END

Monroe

To Snohomish

203

WOODS CREEK

26

Alternate Access

27

RIVER

2

28

SKYKOMISH RIVER

29

(Sultan to Monroe)

30

Ben Howard Road

SKYKOMISH

31

ELWELL CREEK

2

32

START

33

SULTAN RIVER

34

Sultan

Miles

0 1 2

35

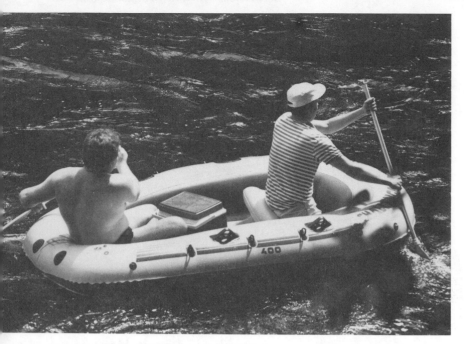

Do not run a river without wearing a PFD.

The west end of the Ben Howard Road is reached by crossing the bridge over the Sky south of Monroe and taking the first left. The access lies 2 miles from the Highway 203 bridge south of Monroe, about 8 from the access in Sultan.

Description. From the launch site at the mouth of the tributary Sultan River (RM 34.4), the Sky flows southwest in a huge open "S" to accept the offerings of Elwell Creek flowing in from the south (RM 31.7). The river is broad and swift, especially just before it reaches the south side of its floodplain against a steep hillside.

From the mouth of Elwell Creek the Sky angles west-by-northwest for 2 miles until it bumps into the ridge carrying U.S. Highway 2 between Monroe and Sultan. This section is well wooded to screen the agricultural lands that flank the Sky through this entire segment. There are broad gravel bars in summer, ideal for lunch stops, and paddlers can pick sun or shade.

From its encounter with U.S. Highway 2, the Sky makes a beeline to the southwest again, running headlong into that same steep hillside, which turns it west-by-northwest again, bouncing it back and forth between its floodplain barriers. In less than a mile the fishermen's access on the left bank offers an out to the weary paddler.

The Sky approaches the highway again in another mile, then turns southwest for a 2-mile run past Monroe, where the take-out lies on the right (north) bank, just below the Highway 203 bridge. Paddlers who have planned a longer run can continue to the confluence of the Sky with the Snoqualmie 4 miles downstream (see Trip #15).

17 *SKYKOMISH RIVER:* *Big Eddy to Sultan*

Location: east of Sultan along U.S. Highway 2
Distance: 9 miles
River Time: 2 to 3 hours
Maps: Sultan (7.5'), Index (15')
Best Season: all year, but especially summer
Hazards: logjams, sweepers, rapids, clay ledges
Shuttle: 8 miles on paved roads
Rating: B+

Overview. The Skykomish River from the Big Eddy beneath the U.S. Highway 2 bridge east of Gold Bar to the small park west of Sultan is a favorite segment for paddlers who like a little action. Most of it comes in the first quarter mile in the form of a Class II rapid that can be seen from the launch site. There are a few other minor rapids and a series of waves, and one chute caused by gray mud ledges about halfway down the run. The adjacent highway and farmlands are unnoticeable, for the most part, and the wildlife is plentiful, a great picnic run with several massive gravel beaches.

Access. The obvious take-out for this run is the small park off U.S. Highway 2 at the west edge of Sultan. The put-in is just south of U.S. Highway 2, 8 miles east at the Big Eddy, a huge, deep green mildly swirling pool. The Big Eddy is visible from the U.S. Highway 2 bridge 2 miles east of downtown Gold Bar.

Driving Directions. To reach the take-out, which lies beneath the railroad bridge adjacent to the U.S. Highway 2 bridge, at the park on the Sultan River just west of Sultan, drive east on U.S. Highway 2 to the edge of Sultan. Turn left into the park immediately east of the Sultan Waste Water Treatment Plant.

To reach the put-in, drive back to U.S. Highway 2, turn left (east), drive through Sultan, Startup and Gold Bar. A mile beyond Gold Bar the highway crosses the Skykomish on a high bridge. Just beyond the

A rafting party stops for lunch on a Skykomish gravel bar.

bridge turn right down a bumpy dirt road to an access on the left bank of the river between the railroad bridge downstream and U.S. Highway 2.

Description. From the Big Eddy, a good place to practice paddling technique, the river dives under the Burlington Northern Railroad bridge, and immediately enters a Class II rapid. Below the rapid, the river doglegs to the right, moving quickly into a second less-severe rapid. (Caution: One canoeist has drowned in the first half mile of this river segment for failing to wear a PFD.)

The river broadens and shallows, becoming a mellow river for the next 3 or 4 miles, its banks lined with tall trees, its waters full of fish that entice fishermen, kingfishers, great blue herons, mergansers and ospreys.

A blue-gray claybank appears on the left, marking a peculiar geologic feature that manifests itself in a series of waves and strange cur-

SKYKOMISH
RIVER
(Big Eddy to Sultan)

rents that have flipped a few canoes. The hard-clay bottom is very near the surface at low water levels, but the water is difficult to read.

A few homes appear along the shore as the river splits around islands; paddlers generally take the right-hand channels. Either of the two big islands at RM 36 and RM 37 will serve as a lunch stop, but the second island is especially popular, summer or winter. It is a great place to skip rocks, and the big logjam offers some protection from the wind if there is any. In the summer it makes a good swimming beach as well.

The Wallace River enters from the right just below the second big island as the river gathers itself together for the parade through town. Numerous houses line the right bank as the river approaches Sultan. After passing beneath the bridge across the Skykomish in Sultan—the one that leads to Ben Howard Road—there is only 0.25 mile to make the landing on the right, just below the mouth of the Sultan River, which makes a tricky landing at times.

18 SNOQUALMIE RIVER: *Duvall to Confluence*

Location: Lower Snoqualmie Valley
Distance: 10 miles
River Time: 3 hours
Maps: Monroe, Maltby (7.5')
Best Season: all year, autumn colors, blackberries
Hazards: none
Shuttle: 12 miles
Rating: A

Overview. The lower Snoqualmie meanders through a lush valley where dairying is king and Holstein cattle provide much of the background noise and smell. However, the final few miles flow through an isolated, heavily forested area reminiscent of a southern swamp. Ideal for summer and early fall paddling—rope swings hang from riverside trees, sandy beaches invite swimming and picnicking, blackberries ripen in August and September—this segment offers placid paddling through private lands (but the river below mean high water is for public use).

Access. The best put-in is from a public fishing area (Taylor's Landing) at the north edge of Duvall on the right bank of the river. The take-out is just below the confluence of the Snoqualmie with the Skykomish beneath the Highway 522 bridge across the Snohomish

Upper Snohomish River access below the Highway 522 bridge.

River (see Trip #15). An alternate take-out at the High Bridge access shortens the trip by about 3 miles.

Driving Directions. To reach the take-out, drive Highway 522 between Woodinville and Monroe to where it intersects the Snohomish-Monroe Road, west of Monroe. Turn east on this road toward Monroe, then turn right (south) almost immediately onto Tester Road and follow it as it roughly parallels Highway 522 southwest toward the Snohomish River.

Tester Road becomes 162nd, then 176th, then 159th, and finally 180th as it weaves its way southwest to pass beneath the Highway 522 bridge over the Snohomish. The rough take-out lies left of the road, on the right bank of the river.

An alternate take-out at the High Bridge public fishing access can be reached by taking the High Bridge Road east off West Snoqualmie Valley Road NE that roughly parallels the river on the west bank and intersects the Woodinville-Duvall Road. High Bridge Road (Tualco Valley) can also be reached from the east off Highway 203 a mile south of Monroe.

To reach the launch site (Taylor's Landing), drive to Duvall in the lower Snoqualmie Valley: 8 miles south of Monroe, 14 miles northwest of Fall City on Highway 203. The Woodinville-Duvall Road reaches Duvall from the west, crossing the Snoqualmie River just before entering town. Turn left onto Highway 203 heading north (toward Monroe) and drive 0.2 mile to the public fishing access left of the highway. This is the launch site.

Description. From Duvall (RM 10) the river is deep, diked and rip-rapped, but placid and peaceful; an easy river to paddle, with little current, ideal for beginning paddlers. The river makes a straight run for a mile north, then doubles back upon itself in a tight "S" at RM 8.7. For the next few miles, it passes through pasturelands (adjacent to dairy farms) on the east side of the valley. At RM 6.2 the river crosses the King-Snohomish County Line.

Nothing much changes on the river in Snohomish County except that the river widens and begins a gradual snaking movement toward the west side of the valley. At RM 3.6 it makes a sharp turn to the north and picks up a little speed around a small island where the river both narrows and shallows. In less than a mile (at RM 2.8) the river passes under High Bridge Road, a possible take-out, then enters its "southern swamp" stage for the next mile or so before breaking out into a lively little riffle less than a mile above the confluence.

The river straightens for its last mile as it runs past the promontory that separates it from the Skykomish; the two rivers run almost parallel for their final mile. Where they join, the Snohomish River is born. Almost immediately they split again around an island created by silt from both rivers. Just below the island, the Highway 522 bridge becomes obvious. The take-out lies on the right bank near the road that creeps beneath the bridge.

19 SNOQUALMIE RIVER:
Fall City to Tolt Mouth

Location: between Fall City and Carnation
Distance: 11 miles
River Time: 4 hours
Maps: Snoqualmie, Fall City, Carnation (7.5')
Best Season: all year except at flood stage
Hazards: pilings in the river, sweepers, logjams
Shuttle: 8 miles
Rating: A

Overview. The Snoqualmie River between Fall City and Carnation is a bucolic stretch of river perfect for novice paddlers. It may be bound by dikes much of the way, but the river is well forested, offers views of its agricultural valley and distant peaks, and gives the beginning paddler few worries. There are a few riffles, sweepers and log-jams, but the current is so slow, for the most part, that they serve as

24

To Duvall
Carnation

Alternate
Access

Suspension
Bridge

END

John MacDonald
Park

TOLT   RIVER

Tolt Hill Road

West Snoqualmie Valley Road

25

26

Carnation
Golf Course

SNOQUALMIE RIVER

(Fall City to Tolt Mouth)

27

28

29

30   203

Miles

0   1   2

32

Tall Chief
Golf Course

31

To
Redmond

33

Alternate
Access

Richter's
Boat
Landing

34

Neal Road

202

SNOQUALMIE RIVER

35

36

START

Fall City

Alternate
Access

SE 44th Pl.

RAGING RIVER

N

202

To
Snoqualmie

To I-90

Riverside rope swings provide summertime play.

good training for more rambunctious river segments. There is an alternate take-out 3 miles into the trip for anyone who wants a shorter run.

Access. There are four accesses: two possible launch sites on the left bank in Fall City about 0.25 mile apart, a boat ramp 3 miles downstream just off Highway 203, and a good take-out at the mouth of the Tolt River near MacDonald Park (King County) at the edge of Carnation.

Driving Directions. To reach the take-out, drive to Carnation on Highway 203 between Fall City and Monroe. Just south of Carnation, at the bridge across the Tolt River, turn west onto a dirt road immediately north of the bridge. This road leads to the mouth of the Tolt, where a convenient rough access offers a reasonable take-out on the right bank just below the Tolt.

A few dozen yards downstream there are possible take-out points beneath the suspension footbridge across the Snoqualmie on the right bank near the parking area in MacDonald County Park. To reach this area, take the turnoff for the park, between Carnation and the Tolt Bridge (north of the Tolt River).

To reach the suggested launch site, drive south on Highway 203 to Fall City, crossing the bridge over the Snoqualmie into town. There are two alternatives: (1) turn right and park along the road within the next few dozen yards—if there is room—and launch from the gravel bar beneath the bridge on river left; (2) keep going straight through Fall City toward Preston. Just after crossing the bridge over Raging River, turn left onto SE 44th Place, which leads to a boat ramp and a campground at the river's edge on the left bank. Either access is a good launch site.

The intermediate alternate access, known as Richter's Landing, lies just off Highway 203, 2.5 miles north of Fall City, at the northern terminus of Neal Road, which has its southern terminus less than 0.25 mile north of the Highway 203 bridge over the Snoqualmie, at the north edge of Fall City. Neal Road roughly parallels the river between the river and Highway 203.

Description. From either Fall City launch site (RM 36.1 or 36.3), the river flows northwest for a little over 2 miles between rip-rapped banks overgrown with blackberry bushes and lined with native vegetation. Adjacent farms go largely unnoticed. There are a few mild riffles and one stretch where old pilings in the river require some maneuvering.

At RM 33.7 the river turns abruptly to the right and in less than a mile passes the boat ramp at Richter's Landing. Highway 203 comes close enough to see from the river twice in the next mile, and there is another area where old pilings create a potential hazard. Farms begin to encroach on the river corridor, and the banks in places are beaten down by cattle.

The river meanders widely for the next several miles, looping back and forth on the west side of the valley, and it comes close to both the Tall Chief Golf Course and the Carnation Golf Course some 5 river miles apart. The river first aims at Tall Chief (RM 31), then runs north for a mile through farmlands. At RM 30 it begins a series of three east-west hairpin bends in the next 2 miles, all through pasture- or crop-lands.

Through most of this segment the river is slow and deep, full of snags and tree trunks anchored in the sandy bottom. At RM 28 it begins a loop to the north, then abruptly south, and finally, northeast for 0.5 mile before it swings west again past Carnation Golf Course (river left). Once more it turns abruptly north in a big bend adjacent to West Snoqualmie Valley Road, and for the last mile of this segment, it flows almost due north to the Tolt Mouth take-out.

Paddlers hug the bank at low water, Snoqualmie River near Fall City.

20 *SNOQUALMIE RIVER: Falls to Fall City*

Location: southeast of Fall City
Distance: 4 miles
River Time: 1 to 2 hours
Maps: Snoqualmie, Fall City (7.5′)
Best Season: all year
Hazards: rapids, especially above Tokul Mouth
Shuttle: 3 miles on paved road, ideal for a bicycle shuttle
Rating: B, upstream travel C

Overview. The Snoqualmie River between Snoqualmie Falls and Fall City is short—about 4 river miles—but it offers good variety. Many experienced paddlers go upstream from the boat launch to play

117

Fall City

202 36 To Carnation

END

RAGING RIVER

203

To I-90

Alternate Access

SE 44th Pl.

Public Boat Launch

Fall City Golf Course

37

38

Fish Hatchery Road

39

202

START

Plum's Landing Public Boat Launch

SNOQUALMIE

SNOQUALMIE RIVER

(Falls to Fall City)

RIVER

Alternate Access

TOKUL

40

CREEK

Powerhouse

N

Snoqualmie Falls

Alternate Access (Kayak)

Miles

0   1   2

in the Class II rapids above (within sight of the falls). Polers like to practice their skills in the rocky rapids of this upper section, but even novice paddlers can negotiate the river downstream (though at low water levels the rapids become rockier and tighter). Blackberries festoon the banks to provide succulent snacks, birdlife is abundant, and fishing is often good.

Access. Excellent access to this segment of river is available at two possible take-outs in Fall City and at the logical put-in, a public fishing access area just below the mouth of Tokul Creek, along Fish Hatchery Road. Kayakers often drive to the end of Fish Hatchery Road, to the power plant at the foot of the falls, and launch from the trail immediately below the powerhouse.

Driving Directions. Drive to Fall City, taking Highway 202 (from the west), Highway 203 (from the north) or Highway 202 (from the south, off I-90 through North Bend and Snoqualmie). To reach the take-out below the bridge in Fall City, turn west just south of the Highway 202/203 bridge (at the junction of Highway 202 and Highway 203). The take-out is under the bridge and can be accessed from roadside parking between the river (left bank) and the road (Highway 202 from Redmond).

To reach the boat ramp 0.25 mile upstream, take Highway 203 south from the junction of Highway 202 and Highway 203, cross the bridge over Raging River, and turn left immediately past the bridge onto SE 44th Place, which follows Raging River to its confluence with the Snoqualmie. The boat ramp lies on the dike left of the river a few dozen yards above the confluence, near the entrance to a riverside campground.

To reach the launch site from Fall City, cross the Highway 203 bridge heading north, turn right immediately, following Highway 202 toward Snoqualmie and North Bend. After a mile, turn right onto Fish Hatchery Road, which angles off Highway 202 toward the river. Follow the road along the river to Plum's Landing Public Boat Launch to the right of the road, on the right bank of the river.

To reach the kayaker's launch area, continue on the same road, cross Tokul Creek, and drive up the hill and around a bend or two to the small parking area by a usually locked gate at the powerhouse. The launch is achieved by following a trail to the river to the right of the fence around the power plant facility.

Description. This segment gets progressively tougher heading upstream from the boat ramp, progressively easier using the kayaker's launch at the powerhouse and heading downstream. Below the boat ramp the river has a couple of mild rapids and a few rocks to dodge at

Negotiating a shallow stretch of riffles, Snoqualmie River below the falls.

low water levels. It becomes a broad river that deepens and slows as it approaches Fall City.

There are a few riffles in low water as the current swings from one side of the river to the other, but once the river flows into its big bend to the right around Fall City Golf Course, it is almost like a lake; a long, narrow stretch of deep green water. The river turns abruptly to the left as it approaches Highway 202 a mile east of Fall City; then hugs that road for the rest of the way. A few ancient pilings line the right bank, and the left bank is busy with the campground, which covers the promontory around which the last bend of the river is made.

The take-out is on the left just above the mouth of Raging River. At this writing, a commonly used rough take-out lies just below the mouth of Raging River, but the land is privately owned and likely to be developed. The take-out below the bridge is also on the left, a few hundred yards below the mouth of Raging River.

21 *SNOQUALMIE RIVER: Above the Falls*

Location: *North Bend to Snoqualmie*
Distance: *3.5 miles*
River Time: *1 to 2 hours*
Maps: *North Bend, Snoqualmie (7.5'), Bandera (15')*
Best Season: *all year*
Hazards: *sweepers, logjams, rapids, major falls downstream*
Shuttle: *4 miles on paved road, ideal for bicycle shuttle*
Rating: *B*

Overview. A river obvious from the road, this section is difficult to get to. It has few real access points, all of which have limited parking. But the river is a real gem, involving all three major forks of the Snoqualmie above the falls. It lies right under Mount Si, which provides a spectacular background for the entire run. The river itself is delightful, with a few riffles, lots of deep pools, a largely natural shoreline, and numerous sand and gravel bars much used by fishermen and picnickers. It is also a favorite for tubers and air-mattress floaters.

Access. Although this segment lies in a mixed rural-urban area with lots of roads in the vicinity, real access to the river is limited. Rough but adequate access lies adjacent to the Mill Pond Road 0.5 mile above the falls, and roadside or trail access is available from Reinig Road. A good but limited launch site lies beneath the bridge on 428th Avenue SE northeast of North Bend.

Driving Directions. To reach the take out, drive east on Highway 202 from Fall City toward Snoqualmie and North Bend. At the top of the falls at the northwest edge of Snoqualmie—just beyond Snoqualmie Falls Lodge and before crossing the Snoqualmie River—turn left onto Mill Pond Road. The take-out lies to the right of the road, just beyond the bend of the river at a small informal access point that may require roadside parking. (A small parking area lies across the road on the north side of Mill Pond Road at the Weyerhaeuser mill.)

To reach the launch site, drive east on Mill Pond Road to SE Reinig Road, which continues upstream alongside the river eastward. SE 396th may seem like the continuation of the main road here, but SE Reinig Road turns right at the next intersection, at a bend of the river where rough access exists on river right at a favorite summer play spot for swimmers and waders.

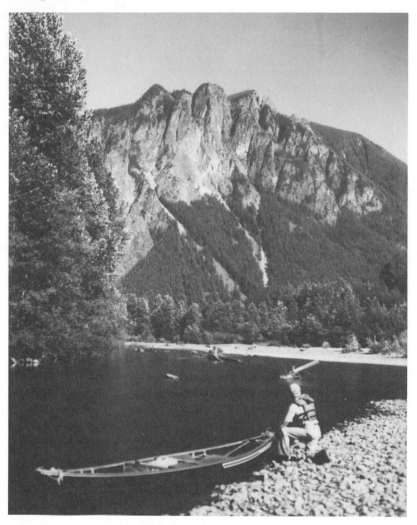

View of Mount Si from the Middle Fork of the Snoqualmie.

Continue east on SE Reinig Road to a "T" intersection, turn right (south) and go 0.6 mile to SE 92nd (a dead-end road) and turn left, then immediately right onto a rough dirt road that leads under the bridge across the Middle Fork. This is the best place to launch, but there is limited parking (space for only two or three vehicles).

Description. At the launch site, the river is pleasant and pictur-esque: Mount Si looms over the paddler's shoulder, and downstream the river is wild in its scenic beauty but mild in its flow. At the first

bend of the river, however, the river turns a bit wild in its flow. After a little jog to the left, it makes a sharp swing to the right against a gigantic logjam that at high water could be a terror. At low flows it is merely a hazard to maneuver past, but there are numerous snags in the sometimes swift water in this first mile.

Just below the logjam, the Middle Fork meets the North Fork head-on and the currents swirl together off a long sandy point bar. With a trail coming into this vicinity on the right, fishermen and picnickers use the area heavily. The deep pools begin just below the confluence with plenty of debris in the river, but the current is so slow that the logs and snags offer few real hazards; they're just obstacles to maneuver around.

Pools and riffles alternate to the mouth of the South Fork on the left, which is totally blocked by fallen trees at this writing. Reinig Road runs along the right bank, offering possible access at a couple of points. A few rural homes line the bank as the river becomes one big, slow, deep channel.

As it turns left in a big bend beneath a railroad bridge, it passes the swimming hole on the right at the junction of SE 396th and Reinig Road, a possible launch or take-out point. Soon the river swings back to the right under a bridge. The edge of the town of Snoqualmie lines the left bank of the river, a thin fringe of timber between the river and Mill Pond Road lines the right.

This slow, deep stretch continues around moderate bends, the river passing under the railroad bridge that serves the Weyerhaeuser mill, and soon the protective railing along Mill Pond Road comes into view—the sign that it is time to look for the take-out on the right, just upstream from the railing.

22 SAMMAMISH RIVER

Location: between Redmond and Kenmore
Distance: 13 miles
River Time: 4 to 5 hours
Maps: Redmond, Kirkland, Bothell (7.5'); NOAA Chart: 18447
  (lower river)
Best Season: all year
Hazards: trash and debris in the river
Shuttle: 12 miles on paved roads and streets, bicycle shuttle ideal
Rating: A

Overview. The Sammamish River, which links Lake Sammamish with Lake Washington, creates a passage between the lakes for boats

Fishing and wading at the mouth of Bear Creek.

as well as for anadromous fish. The Sammamish River Trail runs all the way from Marymoor County Park to Bothell. The river flows slowly through an urban area that supports beaver, muskrats and numerous species of nesting birds, including many ducks and geese. It offers nearby access to fine restaurants, shopping areas and a winery as it passes through Redmond, Hollywood Corner, Woodinville, Bothell and Kenmore.

Access. Abundant access to the Sammamish River suggests numerous short sections of this segment for brief after-work runs. There is easy access in Marymoor County Park and from West Lake Sammamish Parkway south of Redmond, from several points in downtown Redmond, from every bridge crossing in the valley (and there are several), from both sides of the river in Bothell, and at a public boat ramp in Kenmore.

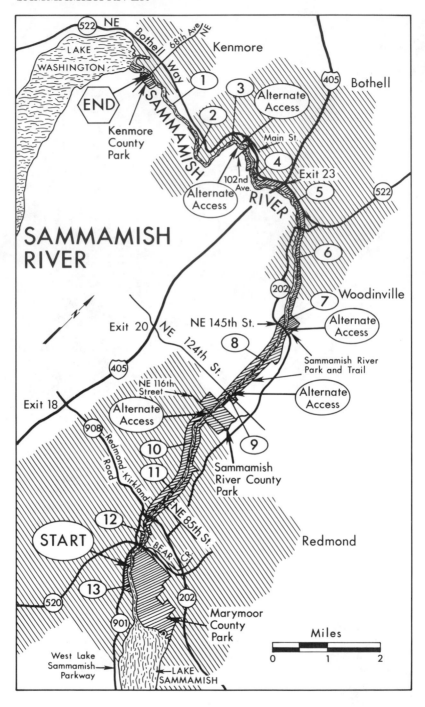

SAMMAMISH RIVER

Additional access is available at several parks on both Lake Sammamish and Lake Washington if a longer run is sought and if paddlers are willing to travel upstream against the usually mild current.

Driving Directions. To reach the last take-out before Lake Washington, take NE Bothell Way (Highway 522), the route that follows the north end of Lake Washington, into Kenmore. At 68th Avenue NE, turn right, cross the Sammamish River, and immediately turn right again into a public fishing access on the left bank of the river beneath the bridge (Kenmore County Park). There is substantial parking here, but the area is heavily used by power boats and is often crowded with vehicles and boat trailers. The nearest auxiliary parking is blocks away.

To reach the Bothell accesses, return to NE Bothell Way (Highway 522) and head east. As it enters Bothell, the road curves left (north). Just as it begins to curve back to the right (east again), turn right onto Wilson Avenue into the park at Bothell Landing, an access on river right with parking and several nice shops and restaurants nearby.

The other Bothell access is just across the river on the left bank. Turn right off Main Street (a block north of NE Bothell Way and Highway 522) onto 102nd Avenue, heading south over the Sammamish River. Take the first right just past the bridge approach on the south side of the river, turning into a large parking area that offers access to the river's left bank—a good take-out or put-in point.

To reach the access points in the Sammamish Valley, retrace the route to Highway 522, which soon becomes a freeway. Turn right toward Woodinville, then take the Woodinville exit and follow Highway 202 south, first along the west side of the river, then along the east side after it crosses the river on NE 145th Street. It is possible to access the river at any of the crossings that intersect with Highway 202—NE 145th Street, NE 124th Street, NE 116th Street (in Sammamish River County Park)—between Woodinville and Redmond.

In Redmond itself it is possible to access the river at several street ends and at NE 85th Street, all of which abut against the Sammamish River Trail. The better accesses, however, lie in Marymoor County Park immediately south of Redmond. These are reached by taking West Lake Sammamish Parkway (Highway 901) south off the Redmond-Kirkland Road (Highway 908).

One access lies between Highway 901 and the river, 0.2 mile south of the red light at the entrance to Marymoor County Park; but it is rough, unpaved and somewhat steep at low water. The better access, though it requires a carry of several dozen yards, lies in the park. Turn right (east) at the red light on Highway 901, follow the main road into Marymoor County Park, turn right toward the Pea Patch, Picnic Area and Dog Training Area. Park in the large parking lot as near the river as possible, and carry the craft to the river (which is swift in this vicinity near the outlet of Lake Sammamish).

SAMMAMISH RIVER

Description. Launching at the outlet of Lake Sammamish requires an upriver carry of a couple hundred yards but gives a swift start on the run to Bothell or Kenmore. Below the fast water, the river swings along the edge of Marymoor County Park adjacent to the Sammamish River Trail, which parallels this segment all the way to Bothell. Bear Creek comes in on the right about a mile below the lake outlet. The river passes beneath the Highway 520 bridge high overhead, enters Redmond, flanked by condominiums, passes under the Redmond-Kirkland Road bridge (Highway 908) and a railroad bridge, then passes an office park and the Redmond City Hall. There are a number of good restaurants within easy walking distance of the river.

Channelized for most of this stretch to Lake Washington, the Sammamish runs northward out of Redmond. However, the fact that it lies in a uniform-sided trough does not detract from its aesthetic quality nor its wildlife and natural beauty. There are views of Mount Rainier upstream, and beaver and muskrats live in this stretch.

Ducks and geese nest here, along with red-winged blackbirds and marsh wrens. There are swallows, spotted sandpipers, northern harriers, red-tailed hawks, kingfishers, killdeer, grebes, great blue and green herons, as well as yellow iris and wild sweetpeas that bloom in summer, cattails and blackberries, ripe in late summer. A few noisy electric pumps drain water from the river in late summer for nearby irrigation.

The water is slow, even sluggish, but there is always a perceptible flow and a sense of the natural. The river passes open meadows, ball fields, turf farms, dairies, scattered condos. It passes within 0.25 mile of rural shopping centers and a major winery. Bikers, runners, fishermen, hikers, skaters, hot air balloons and ultralight planes, even dogsledders (with sleds on wheels) may be seen from the river.

As the river passes the Tolt Pipeline Trail, it swings northwest toward Woodinville, scrapes the edge of that growing community, and turns westward through a light industrial area. Even as it approaches the noisy overpasses that carry I-405 overhead, the river is flanked by small farms and residences. Soon it begins to curve past suburban homes, nurseries, golf courses, and a couple of mobile parks.

The river widens, making room for power boats tied up at private docks, and Canada geese mob the river in this area. Always there is activity along the trail that parallels the river, and the closer the river gets to Bothell, the more the urban environment encroaches upon the natural. The take-out on the left bank in Bothell is a good place to stop after a 10-mile run. Bothell Landing on the right just beyond offers a pleasant park, more urban than bucolic.

The last 2.5 miles are largely urban-industrial, and the power boats ply this stretch so continuously (especially on weekends and after working hours during the week), that it is less than pleasant for paddling. Still it can be delightful in the early mornings and whenever you can have the river to yourself.

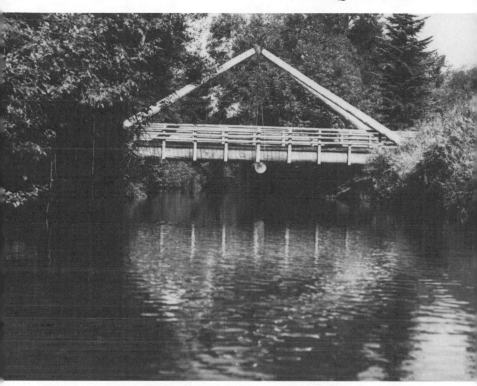

A wooden footbridge over Issaquah Creek.

23 *ISSAQUAH CREEK*

Location: south end of Lake Sammamish, north of Issaquah
Distance: 1 to 2 miles
River Time: 1 to 2 hours
Map: Issaquah (7.5')
Best Season: all year
Hazards: debris from human activity, natural debris
Shuttle: none necessary, 2 miles at most
Rating: A

Overview. One of the smallest streams covered in this book, Issaquah Creek is perhaps the most intimate. It requires no shuttle because it involves paddling up a creek from an access on the lake into which it flows, then returning. The creek offers a natural area in the midst of rapid urban development. It has a salmon run, muskrats, beaver, deer, coyotes, and abundant birdlife, from bald eagles to marsh wrens, from green herons to nesting ducks. It is protected, after a fashion, by Lake Sammamish State Park.

Access. The best access is from the boat launch area at the southeast end of Lake Sammamish in Lake Sammamish State Park. An alternate access, which involves a longish carry, is from the swimming beach area of Lake Sammamish State Park at the south end of the lake.

Driving Directions. Take I-90 east to the second Issaquah exit (Exit #17). Take the East Lake Sammamish Parkway north about 3 miles to the Lake Sammamish State Park boat launch area, turn left into that facility, and launch onto the southeastern lobe of lake Sammamish.

To reach the Lake Sammamish State Park swimming beaches, take I-90 east to the first Issaquah exit (Exit #15), go north 0.25 mile to SE 56th Street, turn left, and after 0.5 mile, turn right into the park entrance. Follow the signs to the swimming beach and park as close as possible, because the carry will be a couple of hundred yards. The area may be crowded in summer.

Description. Between the boat launch at Lake Sammamish State Park southwest and the low-lying delta of Issaquah Creek, a few

In the fall, salmon run this stretch of Issaquah Creek.

power boats may be encountered, but once into the creek mouth and heading upstream, the noise, as well as the wind and most of the people, will be left behind. A few trails in the vicinity may have hikers, but within 0.25 mile (shortly after passing beneath the footbridge across the creek), they too should be left behind.

The channel may be blocked by natural debris from recent storms, but boaters can generally make their way up the creek with either pole or paddle—though the pole may get snagged in overhead vegetation at times, for the river flows through a virtual tunnel of trees and shrubs. Blackberry vines hang over the water in places but can easily be avoided. They can also be sought out for snacks in the late summer or early fall.

The creek winds along through the trees and shrubs, gradually increasing in speed as it breaks into an opening here and there. At a sharp turn on the left about half a mile from the mouth, there is a strong current around a little island that may call for portaging or lining. However, especially with a pole, it is usually possible to work your way upstream. A few fishermen or a pair of lovers may be seen along the bank.

Steep cut-banks a few feet high mark the creek's course through the meadows as it approaches SE 56th Street. In the summer these meadows are full of wildflowers and goldfinches feeding on thistle seeds. In late spring the creek abounds with families of ducks, mostly mallards. Fall brings the salmon runs, fun to watch as they work their way up to the hatchery in Issaquah. Paddlers can turn around at any point and drift back down to the mouth, then paddle across the lake to the launch site, which is also the take-out.

24 CEDAR RIVER

Location: Maple Valley to Renton
Distance: 14.5 miles
River Time: 3 to 4 hours
Maps: Maple Valley, Renton (7.5′)
Best Season: all year, great in summer
Hazards: logjams, sweepers, rapids, one headwall
Shuttle: 12 miles by paved road
Rating: B

Overview. The Cedar River is the one that flows under the Renton Library, the one that can be seen from the I-405 "S" curves. A raging Cascade river in its youth, its final few miles offer an active paddling experience through a bucolic semirural area. The river is small and

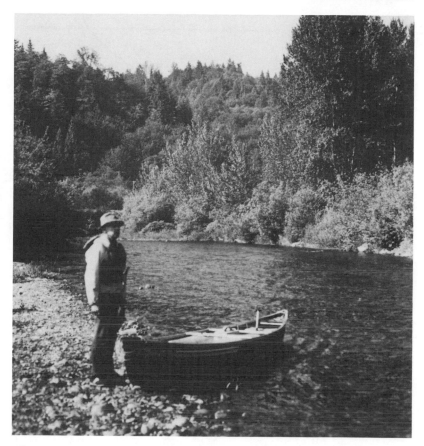

The Cedar River.

intimate, a rocky run with brushy bends, an occasional high bluff, lots of gravel bars, numerous species of birds, including mallards and mergansers, and evidence of beaver and muskrats. Its run through downtown Renton is unique, with anadromous fish visible in the clear cool water, even under the library.

Access. The last mile of the Cedar River before it flows into Lake Washington is flanked on the right by parklands with an excellent take-out across the river from the Renton Airport. The logical launch site is a rough, often-rutted access at the edge of Maple Valley, within sight of the Highway 18 overpass.

Driving Directions. To reach the take-out, find the Cedar River Trail and Park in Renton off North 6th Street from Logan Avenue

North in the midst of the Boeing Complex. NE Park Drive, which becomes Lake Washington Boulevard North, is a good way to get there from Exit 5 off I-405 (Highway 900 to Issaquah goes off at this same exit).

Lake Washington Beach Park, which has abundant parking, is another potential take-out, but it involves paddling a mile across the lower end of Lake Washington (which can be an interesting run through an industrial area).

To reach the launch site at Maple Valley, take the Enumclaw exit off I-405 to the Renton-Maple Valley Highway (Highway 169). Heading east on this route, paddlers can scout much of the river, especially if they take the Jones Road cutoff that crosses the river, parallels it, and recrosses it again well below Maple Valley.

In Maple Valley, turn left off Highway 169 just after crossing the river, then left again into an unpaved, unmarked riverside access between the highway and the railroad tracks. This is the launch site, unpretentious but adequate. It is 12 miles from the I-405 exit.

Description. From the launch site on river left (RM 14.7), the river is fast and rocky. It passes beneath Highway 169 and Highway 18 in quick succession, runs a fast mile through a brushy corridor, then passes under Highway 169 again and the adjacent railroad bridge a mile northwest of Maple Valley (RM 13.5) to run north of the highway for several miles.

The river has a rural flavor. Well-wooded banks hide most, but not all, of the surrounding homes. Some short, simple rapids and the speed of the current keep paddlers busy as the river swings back and forth across its floodplain, at one moment nudging the railroad embankment on the left, at the next nibbling at the base of the bluff on the right, and at one point (near RM 12) driving into the headwall on the right.

The Cedar flows beneath a bridge (McDonald Road) at RM 11.1, parallels the railroad for a few hundred yards, swings back toward the bluff, back again toward the railroad, and repeats this performance to slide beneath the Jones Road bridge at RM 9.3. Just below this point the highway and the railroad, which have been heading north-northwest, turn due west, still paralleling one another quite closely; whenever you near the railroad tracks, the highway is immediately adjacent.

At RM 5.8 there is access off Jones Road on river right in an area that is frequently used during summer months by air-mattress and inner-tube floaters. Jones Road kisses the riverbank between RM 5 and 6. The river flows beneath the western Jones Road bridge at RM 5.3, then becomes more debris-ridden as the gradient mellows. A mile downstream the river curves left under both the railroad and the highway to make a big loop around Maplewood. It remains south of the highway for the rest of its course to Renton, but the railroad crosses to the south side of the river at RM 2.9.

The Cedar River mellows as it approaches Renton, getting slower, a little deeper, less rambunctious. Development intrudes here and there (a sand and gravel works on the left from which silty water trickles into the river, concrete or asphalt banks in places, buildings), but parklands also embrace much of the riverbank in the lower few miles. Once the river passes beneath the twin spans of I-405, the banks are concrete, the scene urban, including the river's passage under the library.

For the last 1.5 miles there will be people watching, waving, having their lunch along the river. Fish can be seen in the river, and gulls overhead, but it is an urban world, and not a bad place to stop for a drink or something to eat. Paddlers could even exit the river at one of the cross streets, but that might tie up traffic—better to go on the last mile to the take-out suggested above.

25 *DUWAMISH RIVER/ WATERWAY*

Location: Fort Dent Park to Elliott Bay
Distance: 12 miles
River Time: 4 to 5 hours
Maps: Seattle South, Des Moines (7.5'); NOAA Charts: 18448, 18449, 18450
Best Season: all year
Hazards: snags, tidal currents, power boats, large ships, a major rapid (Class II) at low tide below Pacific Highway South Bridge (99)
Shuttle: 12 miles on paved roads, city streets, none necessary
Rating: A, T

Overview. The Duwamish River and the waterway at its mouth provide a unique paddling experience, from fast-water chutes when the tide is going out to dodging ocean-going vessels around Harbor Island while admiring views of the Seattle skyline. The Green River becomes the Duwamish just below Fort Dent Park, where the Black River draining out of Lake Washington once joined it. The Lower Duwamish is almost totally industrial, yet it harbors a great blue heron colony, and fishermen still line the low-level Spokane Street bridge to try for a variety of salt- and freshwater fish.

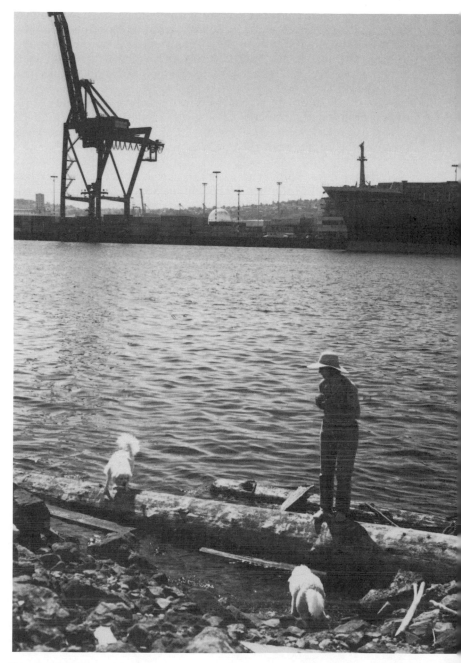

Terminal 30 Access to the lower Duwamish Waterway.

Access. Numerous accesses exist for launching a small paddle craft onto the Duwamish River or Waterway, from the poor put-in at Fort Dent Park on the last mile of the Green (before it becomes the Duwamish) to public access on Elliott Bay, below the artificial saltwater mouth of the river. (It has been totally channelized and its banks have been altered.)

Most of the alternate accesses lie in the saltwater reaches of the river (perhaps more properly called a waterway since it is virtually all paved over and developed). They consist of six public accesses, five of them reached from either East or West Marginal Way.

Driving Directions. The ultimate access—that is, the farthest downstream—is just south of Pier 50 on the Seattle Waterfront. A trip from Fort Dent Park to the Seattle Waterfront makes a run of slightly more than 12 miles.

1. Terminal 30 Access is the lowest one on the river itself, at the lower end of the East Waterway where Alaskan Way South becomes East Marginal Way South. This is south of the Coast Guard Station (south of Massachusetts Street), immediately south of a building marked "GATX" where the huge orange cranes can be seen to the west rising into the sky at the edge of the waterway. Driving south, turn right immediately south of the tank farm (fuel storage structures) at an area marked "Terminal 30, East Waterway, Interim Public Ac-

Seattle, as seen from the lower Duwamish Waterway.

cess Site." This is a Port of Seattle access with ample parking that marks the end of an 11-mile trip from Fort Dent Park.

2. Lower Bridge Site on the east shore of the East Waterway lies a few dozen yards below its split from the West Waterway, but it can be reached only from the eastward traffic on the lower bridge from West Seattle (beneath the new West Seattle bridge). The access ramp is so close to the bridge you can't see it until you are there: immediately after the guard rail ends on the bridge over the East Waterway. There is room for only five vehicles to park at this take-out—the end of a 10-mile trip from Fort Dent Park—or the launch site for local exploring. An outgoing tide causes significant current through the bridge pilings. On high tides there is no clearance beneath the bridge.

3. Diagonal Way Site is probably the best take-out (or launch site, for local exploration) on the entire waterway. There is plenty of parking, and the access is protected by a small indentation at the southwest end of Diagonal Way. Launch along the fence at the south edge to protect fragile intertidal habitat. The turnoff to Diagonal Way is the second stop light south of the viaduct carrying Old Highway 99. It is located just opposite the lower (downstream) end of Kellogg Island.

4. South River Street Site consists of a boat ramp almost directly beneath the First Avenue South Viaduct, just south of the South Michigan Street ramp onto the viaduct. Turn west onto South River Street, a very short street that bisects East Marginal Way a block south of South Michigan. The boat ramp, but little parking, is just east of the Viaduct over the Duwamish. This take-out point serves to terminate an 8-mile trip from Fort Dent Park.

5. Terminal 105 Site lies on the west bank of the Duwamish just as the West Waterway splits around Harbor Island. Located off West Marginal Way, it is a tiny park provided by the Port of Seattle. Just north of Southwest Dakota Street, this access is marked "Duwamish Public Access—Public Shore." A trip from Fort Dent Park ending here would be 10 miles long. (This access is not intended as a boating access, but it can serve that purpose.)

The sixth public access is the one at Fort Dent Park (RM 11.7), which is no more than a trail leading to a sandy beach (at low water levels), or an eddy (at high flows). To reach Fort Dent, get on I-5 any of several different ways: (1) West Seattle Freeway, (2) Old Highway 99, or (3) East Marginal Way. Travel toward Southcenter or the juncture of I-5 with I-405. East Marginal Way (also Highway 181) may be the best bet because it puts you on Interurban Avenue, which crosses Southcenter Boulevard at the right place: at the left turn to Fort Dent Park. Heading south on I-5, take the Interurban exit (Exit 156) and follow Interurban to the Southcenter Boulevard junction and turn left.

Crossing the lower Green River, enter Fort Dent Park and turn left to park at the south end of the parking area adjacent to an open field.

The access is on the point of land at the south edge of the park where the river loops back in a great horseshoe. Check it out on foot before carrying the craft and gear all over the park looking for the right place.

Description. From the launch site in Fort Dent Park the river heads northwest, skirting the park and forming its western boundary. The left bank of the river thinly veils development with a fringe of trees. Within a mile a slough comes in from the right, all that remains of what was once the Black River, the historical outlet of Lake Washington. The confluence of the Green and the Black historically created the Duwamish, named for an Indian tribe that no longer exists.

For the next 2 miles—to the I-5 crossing—the Duamish meanders through Foster Golf Links, a lovely run and a good access site as well. At the I-5 crossing overhead there is traffic noise. If the tide is going out, there is a strong pull by the river, gurgling past snags anchored in the muddy bottom. Earlington County Park embraces the right bank. There are bridges galore: 42nd Avenue South, East Marginal Way (Highway 181), Pacific Highway. Some of this stretch of river is lovely, almost isolated by the dikes raised to control its flooding. Beware of commercial traffic on the river. Groups of paddlers should stay together along one shore or the other.

From RM 5 the Duwamish is an industrial river, but nonetheless interesting and paddle-worthy. Late in the afternoon and on weekends and holidays it can be a delightful place to explore, though power boats often create an atmosphere less than desirable for paddle craft. At RM 0.8 the Duwamish splits around Harbor Island, creating a pair of busy waterways where paddling may not seem appropriate during the working day, but where it can offer unique paddling opportunities.

26 LOWER GREEN RIVER

Location: Kent to Tukwila
Distance: 6.5 miles
River Time: 2 hours
Maps: Renton, Des Moines (7.5′)
Best Season: all year
Hazards: none
Shuttle: 8 miles on paved roads, city streets
Rating: A

Overview. This is a short stretch of placid but relatively fast water bound by dikes on both sides. A worthwhile segment to consider, much of it is flanked by parklands, both in west Kent and in Tukwila.

It begins in a rural area marked by nurseries, berry fields and old barns; traverses Tukwila's industrial and commercial heart; then ends at Fort Dent Park after passing beneath I-405. It provides a link between the Green River in the Auburn-Kent area and the Duwamish River, allowing a continuous trip of more than 30 miles.

Access. Access is limited to the take-out at Fort Dent Park (RM 11.7) and a choice of two possible put-ins almost opposite one another (RM 18.1 and 18.3) in west Kent, just south of South 212th Street.

Driving Directions. Take the Highway 181/Interurban Avenue exit from I-405 (Exit 1) a mile east of the I-5/I-405 interchange and head north on Interurban. Turn right onto Southcenter Boulevard (see map #25) which crosses the lower Green as it enters Fort Dent Park. Turn left at the first intersection in the park and stop as far south and as close to the open field on the southwest as possible. The take-out lies at the bend of the river a hundred yards below the bridge but is reached by a long carry from the south parking area. (See map for Trip # 25).

To reach the put-ins retrace the route to I-405 but do not get back on the freeway. Go straight ahead on Highway 181 (Interurban Avenue, which soon becomes West Valley Road South) heading south. It touches bends of the river at three points and parallels it for several hundred yards, it can be scouted from the road. Turn right at South 212th Street in Kent, and follow it to the river.

To launch on the east side of the river, turn left onto Russell Road just before reaching the river and follow the river south to Van Doren's Landing, the best access on the river in this vicinity. To launch on the west side of the river, cross the Green, turn left onto Frager Road, and follow the river south to an unmarked access around the bend and upstream of Van Doren's Landing. A 4-wheel drive vehicle can get you closer to the river, but it's a short carry either way. There is also an access a mile above I-405 on the west shore near RM 13.

Description. The Green is usually clear in the area of both launch sites, swift and sandy-bottomed. Its grassy dike blocks out much of the surrounding development, but there are domestic geese in the river and enough wild birds to make it worth the effort for birdwatchers. The river meanders in slow, easy curves, passing beneath bridges at South 212th Street and South 176th Street, where it begins a brief love affair with West Valley Road, which it hugs for half a mile.

Christensen Road embraces the left (west) bank. A greenbelt park then a Bicentennial park help preserve the natural aspect of this stretch of river as it cuts through industrial back yards and commercial enterprises. A major manufacturer of paddle craft has its headquar-

The Green River flows through a protected parkway in Tukwila.

GREEN
RIVER
(Lower and
Middle Reaches)

ters less than a quarter mile from the river as it swings back and forth just west of Longacres Race Track, approaching I-405.

After passing beneath the freeway, the lower Green leaves behind much of the developed world and takes on a more natural tone as it approaches Fort Dent Park. It makes a big horseshoe bend, flows beneath the bridge that leads into the park, and bends to the right; the take-out appears on the right just around the bend.

27 GREEN RIVER: *Middle Reach*

Location: Auburn area to West Kent
Distance: 15.6 miles
River Time: 4 to 5 hours
Maps: Des Moines, Renton, Auburn (7.5′)
Best Season: all year
Hazards: logjams, sweepers in upper mile
Shuttle: 15 miles, paved roads
Rating: upper mile, B; remainder, A

Overview. The Green River from the mouth of Big Soos Creek 2 miles above Auburn through West Kent changes from a rural river, where steelhead fishermen dominate the scene, to a suburban river that nibbles the edges of two towns, Auburn and Kent, while following a natural course through agricultural lands and residential fringes. Much of the riverbank is rip-rap overgrown with blackberry bushes, natural grasses and shrubs, ideal habitat for the many species of birds that live here.

Access. Several rough accesses exist between the proposed launch site opposite the mouth of Big Soos Creek 2 miles above Auburn and the proposed take-outs in West Kent, but most of them are in the Auburn vicinity. Adequate public access in or near downtown Kent is badly needed for appropriate utilization of this segment.

Driving Directions. To reach the proposed take-outs in West Kent, find Highway 181 south of I-405 (Exit 1), go south on West Valley Road (Highway 181) to South 212th Street, and turn right (west). At the Green River bridge, either (1) turn left onto Russell Road east of the river to Van Doren's Landing, or (2) turn left onto Frager Road west of the river to an unobtrusive, unmarked access left of the road on the left bank of the river.

The Green River's course through Auburn.

To find any of the suggested launch sites, go back to South 212th, turn right (east) back to Highway 181, turn right again (south) to Highway 516 (Kent-Des Moines Road South), and either (1) turn left to Highway 167 heading south to Auburn, where you take Highway 18, a freeway of sorts, to the proposed launch site; or (2) turn left, then go straight ahead under the Highway 167 overpass on West Meeker Street to Central Avenue in downtown Kent, turn right, go south to 259th Street, and turn left onto what becomes the Green River Road east of the river.

Green River Road offers several possible rough access points as it parallels the river upstream (south) toward Auburn. Isaac Evans Park at the northeast edge of Auburn is one of these points. This route into Auburn has the advantage of permitting the river to be scouted from the road.

The proposed launch site can be reached either by continuing along the Green River Road into Auburn until it becomes 104th Avenue SE, turning right (west) onto SE 320th, which becomes 8th Street NE after crossing the Green River. By weaving around through Auburn—taking Harvey Road south to Main, Main east to R Street SE, and following it until it becomes the Auburn-Black Diamond Road—paddlers can reach the proposed launch site described below.

To reach the proposed launch site from Highway 18, turn right about 3 miles east of Auburn at the exit to the Auburn-Black Diamond Road. Just before that road crosses the Green River, turn right onto the road to Flaming Geyser State Park (SE Green Valley Road), then left into a public fishing access just upstream from the bridge carrying the Auburn-Black Diamond across the Green River. The launch site is on the left bank.

Description. Big Soos Creek's entering the Green River from the right is the first notable natural feature, but two man-made structures dominate the first couple of hundred yards: the Auburn-Black Diamond Road bridge, the Burlington Northern Railroad bridge and the Highway 18 bridge. The first mile of river seems like wilderness with natural islands and forest debris (sunken logs, stumps, sweepers and logjams). The river swings to the left around a bend full of downed trees. At times the river may be entirely blocked, but a portage around the obstacle is usually short and simple, especially at low water.

The river runs into the rip-rapped railroad embankment to the south as it gathers itself into one channel for an "S" turn at the eastern edge of Auburn. Soon houses begin to appear on the left bank, though the right bank remains forested. The diked banks are overgrown with blackberry bushes, natural grasses and shrubs. Bird life abounds: great blue herons, spotted sandpipers, kingfishers galore, several species of swallows, many mallards and mergansers, frequently with young in late spring and early summer.

The trip through east Auburn is delightful, as one of the nicer parts of town smiles on the river (rather than turning its back on the river as Kent seems to). The river flows beneath the Porter Bridge (8th Street NE and SE 320th Street), loops past an undeveloped park (Isaac Evans) on the right bank, where access to the river is possible, then north out of town past Brennan Park on the left and the Auburn Golf Course on the right.

Between Auburn and Kent the river is much used by tubers, rafters and air-mattress floaters who gain access from Green River Road east of the river. The river is clear and shallow with a few riffles and some deep pools, an ideal poling stream. The banks are natural enough to attract such bright-colored birds as orioles, goldfinches, and western tanagers.

In 2.5 hours from the proposed launch site, a paddler can reach Kent at the intersection of 78th Avenue South and South 259th Street. But there is no real access even though you can read the street signs from the river; a pity, for the paddler gets hungry and thirsty about this time, and South Kent stores suffer the loss of potential business. Tall grass and blackberry bushes dominate the landscape, and it is possible to discern a small dairy farm.

Below the Highway 167 bridge, the Green is largely a big ditch, but it is a delightful ditch, its banks covered with eye-pleasing vegetation, its waters full of fish (salmon and steelhead), wildlife (beaver and muskrats) and birds. Domestic ducks and geese join their wilder cousins, while hikers, cyclers and joggers join the parade along riverside trails. The take-out on the left at RM 18.5 lies a few hundred yards downstream from Cottonwood Grove. Van Doren's Landing lies a few hundred yards downstream on the right bank at RM 18.2.

28 GREEN RIVER: Yo-Yo Stretch

Location: east of Auburn, Flaming Geyser State Park to the Whitney Bridge
Distance: 3 miles
River Time: less than an hour
Map: Black Diamond (7.5′)
Best Season: all year
Hazards: Class II rapid, logjams
Shuttle: less than 2 miles on paved roads
Rating: B+

Overview. A short and varied section of river, this segment is known to local paddlers as the Yo-Yo Stretch because it is a favorite with paddlers who make the same run down and up, several times a day for practice. It is ideal for poling. Polers can work their way up from the Whitney Bridge into the park and back down again in 2 hours for a good workout. It has small rapids, one short but serious Class II rapid, one interesting bedrock riffle, and a few deep pools with fine beaches and well-forested banks.

Access. There is excellent access at the Whitney Bridge take-out and at several places within Flaming Geyser State Park. One or two roadside accesses are also possible, and with special permission, a few private accesses—all within a very short run.

Driving Directions. From Highway 18 about 3 miles east of Auburn, take the same exit that would lead to the launch site for Trip #27—or take the Auburn-Black Diamond Road out of Auburn, heading east. Just before the road crosses the Green River, turn right onto

Paddlers without PFDs, Green River, Flaming Geyser State Park.

Southeast Green Valley Road. Signs suggest this is the way to Flaming Geyser State Park.

Eight miles from the turnoff, turn right onto SE 219th Street. Within a hundred yards turn right into the parking area at Whitney Bridge Park. Leave a shuttle vehicle—possibly a bicycle (locked to a pole)—here.

To reach the put-in, retrace the route to Southeast Green Valley Road and turn right, continuing toward Flaming Geyser State Park. The road crosses a bridge in less than a mile and then enters the park. Follow the road to its end, park and explore the area for river access. The river is to the north; there are several points along a half mile of riverfront where a craft may be launched.

Description. From any of the launch sites in Flaming Geyser State Park the stream is clear with just enough action to keep paddlers on their toes. In midsummer it is crowded with tubers and sunbathers, kids floating on air mattresses and riverside picnickers. Drifting through the park, boaters pass a few rock gardens and mild rapids, occasional beaver cuts, and during the fishing season, frequent steelheaders, fishermen after the prize gamefish of the Northwest.

At the big bend of the river above Flaming Geyser Bridge there is a deep pool, so deep that even in the clear water you cannot see the bottom. A rope tied to an overhanging tree tells of summer swimming

Horses on the Yo-Yo stretch of the Green River.

GREEN RIVER
(Yo-Yo Stretch)

Whitney Bridge

END

SE 219th Street

SE

42

Flaming Geyser Bridge

Alternate Access

43

Green

44

Flaming Geyser State Park

START

RIVER

45

46

GREEN

Valley

Road

Miles

0   1

here. A long rock garden—merely shallow water at highwater flows—leads to the bridge. Immediately below the bridge there is an exposed gravel-and-sand bar at river left, a swimming beach in the summer and a year-round take-out for those who want to go up and do it again.

Below the bridge the river splits around a series of islands, the flow on either side runnable at any level above absolutely low water. At low water levels it can be shallow and the current can take a craft into sweepers along the shoreline. Around the bend is a small rapid, followed by a deeper section of river, then a bedrock area where the river shallows over sandstone and mud. It drops again into a deep pool, then shallows out, deepens around a bend visible from the road, and gets ready for an honest Class II rapid.

The head of the rapid can be seen but it can't really be scouted from the road. The river splits around a small island, at least at higher water levels, and drops a few feet in 50 yards over a bouldery stretch of fast water. It can be lined on the right from a point that serves as a good scout. Stop and have a look at it if you are uncomfortable with the rapid, but it is fairly straightforward. It is tough to pole up.

From the foot of the rapid to the take-out bridge, the river is broad and shallow, ideal for poling. The take-out is under the bridge, on river right within a 100-foot carry of the parking area.

The river from this access to the mouth of Soos Creek just east of Auburn is a 7-mile Class II run through a rural valley full of horse farms and pastureland, a delightful trip that will challenge beginning paddlers. The river is lined with huge trees and offers excellent habitat for birds and other wildlife as well as excellent fishing.

29 *NISQUALLY RIVER DELTA/ McALISTER CREEK*

Location: between Olympia and Tacoma
Distance: 8 miles combined
River Time: 3 to 4 hours
Maps: Nisqually (7.5'), Anderson Island (15'); NOAA Charts: 18440, 18445, 18448
Best Season: all year
Hazards: logjams, contrary tides, fog, storms
Shuttle: none necessary, up to 10 miles on paved roads
Rating: B, T

Overview. The Nisqually Delta, one of the richest wildlife habitats in Puget Sound, is protected as the Nisqually National Wildlife Refuge. Two major streams—McAlister Creek and the Nisqually River—that created the delta offer unique paddling experiences. More than 200 species of birds have been seen in the refuge, which also harbors numerous species of mammals, reptiles, amphibians and fish, as well as such saltwater species as crabs, clams and oysters, even seals. McAlister Creek, once known as Medicine Creek, was the site of early Indian treaties in western Washington.

Access. Luhr Beach on Puget Sound is the nearest public boat launch. It offers access to both McAlister Creek, which flows past it, and the mouth of the Nisqually itself, a mile or so across the tidal flats. Access to the lower Nisqually is available at RM 3.3 and 3.7 from public boat accesses just upstream from the twin I-5 bridges, one off Old Nisqually Road, the other off 6th Avenue SE at the north edge of Nisqually.

A duck-hunting blind "graces" the Nisqually Delta.

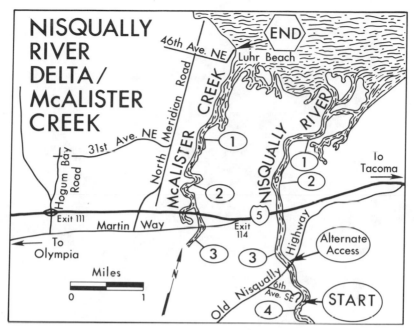

Driving Directions. To reach Luhr Beach take Exit 111 (Yelm-Marvin Road) off I-5 between Tacoma and Olympia, and head north toward Tolmie State Park. In only 0.1 mile turn right onto Hogum Bay Road, then, in less than a mile, turn right onto 31st Avenue NE. After 1.3 miles turn left onto North Meridian Road heading north. In another mile turn right onto 46th Avenue NE, and follow the public fishing signs that direct you to turn left onto D'Milluhr Road, then right to Luhr Beach. The Nisqually Beach Nature Center also resides here.

A simpler way to reach Luhr Beach is to take Exit 114 off I-5 just west of the Nisqually River crossing. Turn right to follow Martin Way west toward Lacey, turn right onto Meridian Road, then follow the signs to the public fishing access, which is Luhr Beach.

To reach the access on the lower Nisqually at RM 3.3, take Exit 116 off I-5 and head for Nisqually. Just before crossing the Nisqually River, turn right into an unmarked public fishing area (rough and unmaintained) that offers access to the right bank of the Nisqually immediately downstream from the Old Nisqually Highway bridge.

To reach the access at RM 3.7 return to the Old Nisqually Highway and turn right, cross the river and continue for 0.5 mile to 6th Avenue SE (marked by a public fishing access sign), turn left and go to the end of the road, where a public handicapped fishing area lies on the left bank of the Nisqually. The parking area is 0.1 mile from the access.

The Nisqually National Wildlife Refuge.

Description. Launching at RM 3.7 poses an immediate problem in the form of a nasty logjam on the left bank, into which the whole river seems to flow at low water. (This minor rapid can be, and perhaps should be, lined at low water.) At higher flows there is plenty of room to negotiate on the right of what becomes a mere riffle. A few residential backyards line the river bank, largely ignoring what the river has to offer. In less than 0.5 mile the river flows beneath the Old Nisqually Highway bridge, and another access lies on the right bank at RM 3.3.

From this point the river is tidal and mellow with a few riffles at low tide. The houses disappear as an Indian fishing camp appears; the tribe for whom the river is named still fishes the streams in accordance with the Medicine Creek Treaty of 1854, signed on what is now McAlister Creek only a few miles away. The twin spans of the I-5 bridge loom ahead as the roar of freeway traffic intrudes into the river corridor, but not for long.

The river slows, both banks are wooded, and the river takes on a mellow mood, creates a placid presence that one paddle partner suggested "could be in Gillford, Connecticut." Soon the protection of the Nisqually National Wildlife Refuge makes its impact; the world grows still, natural, wholesome, and the sound of freeway traffic subsides.

Depending upon the tide level, the river may be tearing along to reach the Sound or backed up in a slow lake, but the setting is pleasant, calm, quiet except for the sounds of nature—or an occasional power boat carrying Indian fishermen to set or check their nets. There are gulls overhead, mallards and wood ducks in the eddies. A trail along the left bank spawns people, bird watchers hiking through the refuge. Blackberry bushes and beaver cuts mark the shoreline; Indian gill nets mark the river's surface.

Soon the craft reaches the open water of the Sound. A seal's head pops up. Duck blinds appear—yes, hunting is allowed on the refuge, but gunners are required to use nontoxic shot and only during the open season. The dock at Luhr Beach is visible to the west. Shore birds and many ducks and geese frequent the area; bald eagles, great blue herons and numerous gulls feed on the mud flats and in the nearby Sound.

The mouth of McAlister Creek can be reached by paddling a few hundred yards west; and if the tide is right, paddling upstream is not difficult. The lower creek is broad, but a mile upstream it narrows and begins to meander, nuzzling the west bank where a steep, forested hillside turns it back to loop through the meadows to the east. The tide mark shows on the vegetation; salt burn kills leaves of vine maple but doesn't seem to bother the sturdy trees that grow right to the water's edge.

It is possible to paddle or pole right up McAlister Creek to I-5, though the outgoing tide creates a fierce flow in the channelized creek where it has been forced by humankind to loop around the bridge supports. Above the I-5 bridge there will be placid water (if the tide charts have been used wisely), but having left the refuge behind , the river is now in agricultural land. It may be best to head back downstream to the take-out at Luhr Beach.

The Chehalis River.

30 *LOWER CHEHALIS RIVER AND SLOUGHS*

Location: Montesano to Hoquiam-Aberdeen-Cosmopolis area
Distance: 13.3 miles
River Time: 3 to 4 hours
Maps: Montesano (15'), Aberdeen, Hoquiam (7.5'); NOAA Chart 18502
Best Season: all year, but best in summer months
Hazards: contrary tides, big ships, power boats
Shuttle: 15 miles on paved roads, none necessary
Rating: A, T

Overview. The lower Chehalis and its associated sloughs combine a logging town and seaport with some amazingly pristine backwater paddling. The lower 3 miles of the river is almost totally urban, commercially developed and export-oriented; but above the 3-mile mark, six sloughs branch off into picturesque bayous reminiscent of Southern swamplands except for the vegetation, which is strictly Northwestern. Three major tributaries covered by this book enter the Chehalis in this segment: the Hoquiam, the Wishkah and the Wynoochee.

Access. Several boat launches provide abundant access to the lower Chehalis: one on the Aberdeen waterfront, another across the Chehalis from the mouth of the Wishkah. a third at RM 3, and a fourth 1 mile south of Montesano just above the mouth of the Wynoochee. Paddle craft access can also be negotiated from Morrison Waterfront Park at RM 1 just below the mouth of Elliott Slough, the only one of seven sloughs that joins the river below RM 3.

Driving Directions. To reach the western-most access, take U.S. Highway 101 (Sumner Street) west through Aberdeen. After entering Hoquiam, turn left (south) onto 28th Street to the Port of Grays Harbor boat ramp (gravel) by the Observatory (hours 7 A.M. to dusk).

To reach the boat ramp across from the mouth of the Wishkah, take U.S. Highway 101 south across the bridge over the Chehalis River (a sign says "to Westport and Raymond"). Turn left at the first stop light (H Street; the main flow of traffic goes left at this light) and left again onto Boone Street as the road bends right just before the South Aberdeen Fire Station appears on the left. (This is an awkward turn in heavy traffic; it may be best to go beyond it, turn around somewhere, and approach it from the other direction so that a right turn is called for.) This is the old West Bridge approach. There is no sign, no dock, and little parking.

To reach the third access in south Cosmopolis, return to U.S. Highway 101 and turn left past the South Aberdeen Fire Station, toward Raymond. Turn left at F Street and drive to the waterfront access provided by Weyerhaeuser.

To reach the boat ramp south of Montesano, return to U.S. Highway 101. At this point there are two options: (1) turn left and continue toward Raymond, but turn left in a few miles on Highway 107 to Montesano on the South Bank Road. This location provides a look at Blue Slough and Preachers Slough, both south of the river. After Highway 107 forks left and crosses the Chehalis River 0.1 mile above the mouth of the Wynoochee River, turn right at a public fishing access sign into a parking area with a boat ramp.

Or (2) turn right and return to Aberdeen, turning right again in downtown Aberdeen onto U.S. Highway 12, heading east. At Montesano, turn right onto Highway 107, drive a mile south of town, past a lumber mill, and turn left into the public fishing access, which is the launch site.

Morrison Waterfront Park, another launch site, is located at what was the dock for the local fishing fleet until 1956. Traveling east on Wishkah Street (U.S. Highway 12), turn right onto Fleet Street just past the shopping mall at the east end of Aberdeen, just before U.S. Highway 12 starts to climb the hill east of town. This area offers access to the right bank of the Chehalis less than 0.25 mile above the mouth of the Wishkah.

Raccoon tracks along a Western Washington riverbank.

Description. The Chehalis is tidal throughout this segment, a big, deep river impacted by logging activities and heavily used by power boats, many of which launch at the boat ramp south of Montesano at RM 13.3. Launching here, paddlers immediately pass beneath the Highway 107, then under the railroad bridge. The Wynoochee enters on the right, flushing the Chehalis with fresh mountain water.

The river flows southwest until it bumps into the railroad embankment (RM 11.6). Then it hugs that embankment for a mile before swinging slowly toward the north and encountering sloughs on the right: first Peels at RM 9.5, then Higgins at RM 8.7. The river narrows, divides around an island (RM 8), and swings toward the south again.

At RM 6.8 Preachers Slough enters from the left (offering a side trip of more than 2 miles up the slough if the tide is high and there are no barriers), and at RM 6.4 Blue Slough enters, also from the left (a side trip of nearly 3 miles up this one). Below Blue Slough the river enters a tight "S" bend that takes it 1.5 miles to complete. Mox Chuck Slough enters from the right at RM 4.4 as the river bends left. The river straightens as it enters Cosmopolis (the Weyerhaeuser mill is visible on the left bank) and greets one more small slough on the left.

Slough exploring can take a lot of time. Just be aware that such side trips add to paddle time. Keep in mind too that tidal influence will alter tour time on the river; it is slow going against an incoming tide, but fair time can be made paddling upstream with the tide.

From RM 3 the river is flanked on the left by the back yards of Cosmopolis, on the right by log export activities and facilities. The river here heads north and then makes a sharp left turn as Elliott Slough enters on the right at RM 1.3. Elliott Slough is largely a log-storage facility, and the Chehalis River from this point is totally engulfed by Aberdeen. In another mile the river gives up its ghost to Grays Harbor.

Pilings in the West Fork of the Hoquiam River.

31 *HOQUIAM RIVER:* *East and West Forks*

Location: Hoquiam and Aberdeen, north of Hoquiam
Distance: 5 miles, East Fork; 9 miles, West Fork
River Time: 2 hours, East Fork; 3 hours, West Fork
Maps: Hoquiam (7.5'), Humptulips (15'); NOAA Chart: 18502
Best Season: all year, but rainy in winter
Hazards: contrary tides, waterfront traffic at end
Shuttle: 7 miles, East Fork; 9 miles, West Fork on paved roads
Rating: A, T

Overview. The Hoquiam River proper, only 2.5 miles long, is totally urban, but at the point where it splits into an East and West Fork, it becomes almost rural, nearly primitive. Both forks have lives and accesses of their own as they loop widely back and forth in sinuous curves through marshy lands that protect the rivers from greater development. They offer peaceful paddling on tidal waters that are disturbed only by such commercial activities as log storage (more historical than current) and sports fishing.

Access. The most logical take-out access is on the Grays Harbor Waterfront in southwestern Aberdeen. Developed boat launches exist on both major forks of the river and on the Little Hoquiam (see Trip #32), from U.S. Highway 101 on the West Fork and from East Hoquiam Road on the East Fork.

Driving Directions. To reach the waterfront take-out in southwestern Aberdeen, turn south from U.S. Highway 101 as it goes through Aberdeen onto 28th Street and head south past a log storage yard to the Observatory, a pointer to the Port of Grays Harbor boat ramp, which is the take-out. This boat ramp is only a few hundred yards east of the mouth of the Hoquiam River.

To reach major access points on the West Fork, go back to U.S. Highway 101 (Lincoln Street) and follow it north out of town toward either of two put-in points: (1) only 2.4 miles north of the ancient steam engine at Last Spur Park in north Hoquiam, turn onto a spur road that veers off to the right (known locally as "Fairfield Acres Access," but unsigned), then turn right again down a residential road, and drive to its dead end, where a log boom serves as a possible public put-in at RM 5.3; (2) five miles north of Last Spur Park, right of the highway, there is a facility known as Green Banks dedicated to public fishing access by ITT Rayonier, Trout Unlimited, and the Northwest

Steelheaders Association (complete with parking and a covered picnic table).

To reach a boat ramp at RM 4.6 on the East Fork (7 miles from the mouth of the Hoquiam), go back to U.S. Highway 101 from the 28th Street take-out, follow it west to 16th Street (a few blocks after the highway begins to parallel the left bank of the Hoquiam River). Turn right (sign says "Woodlawn") onto 16th Street, which soon becomes Broadway, and follow it through Woodlawn, turning right onto East Hoquiam Road, which follows the river, more or less, to a boat ramp 5 miles from the turnoff from 101.

Description. Both forks of the Hoquiam offer interesting and contrastive paddling, both are tidal throughout these segments, and both can be paddled or poled both upstream and down if tidal charts are consulted and followed.

From the boat ramp on the **East Fork**, the river is lined by mud banks at low tide; at high tide, by brushy shorelines with occasional stands of tall trees, even in this heavily cut-over logging land. Fisherman traffic attests to the aquatic life, as do kingfishers and great blue herons. There are a few homes along the bank, a number of pilings

The great blue heron is an omnipresent fisherman on Western Washington rivers.

from earlier log storage areas, and more commercial development downstream as the river meanders through a marshy floodplain.

At RM 2.7 the river kisses the road, as it does again at RM 1.5. At RM 0.5 commercial development begins in the form of forest products and industrial facilities on the left bank. The East Fork joins the West Fork at the north edge of Hoquiam 2.5 miles from Grays Harbor. From RM 0.5 on the East Fork, paddlers are still 3 miles from the waterfront take-out.

The **West Fork** plays hide-and-seek with U.S. Highway 101 from the put-in at RM 9 to RM 3, only 0.5 mile above the confluence of the east and west forks at the north edge of Hoquiam. It is probably more heavily fished than the East Fork because of its proximity to the major highway and the developed fishing facilities. But for all of its access, it is still a pretty primitive paddle; few boats make use of it.

For its first two miles it parallels the highway, passing between towering trees and along shrub-lined banks. Its Middle Fork joins it from the left just above RM 7 opposite the entrance of Bernard Creek from the right.

The river moves away from the highway below RM 7, swinging back to parallel the highway for nearly a mile (RM 6.5 to RM 5.7) before making the big loop on which access #1 is located on the right bank. It loops back near the highway at RM 4.8, then takes a long loop to the east side of its marshy floodplain before making one more move toward the highway to parallel it coming into town at RM 3. Here the Little Hoquiam joins it from the right.

Half a mile below its entry into Hoquiam, it is joined by the East Fork from the left. Totally tidal and surrounded by commercial and residential development for its last 2.5 miles, the Hoquiam flows into Grays Harbor at the west end of Rennie Island. To reach the take-out, paddle 0.5 mile to the Observatory on the Hoquiam waterfront.

32 LITTLE HOQUIAM RIVER

Location: west of Hoquiam
Distance: 3 miles
River Time: 2 to 3 hours
Map: Hoquiam (7.5′); NOAA Chart: 18502
Best Season: all year, but lots of rain in winter
Hazards: contrary tides, power boats
Shuttle: none necessary
Rating: A, T

Overview. This small river may be badly clear-cut at this writing, but its atmosphere suggests *wild* and its waters are full of life. Its ac-

The placid Little Hoquiam serves as a reflection pond.

cess is from an isolated little park, and its upstream reach offers one of the most peaceful experiences paddlers could seek. Even though a new road and bridge have been built over its first fork, many nearby sounds are blocked off by the ridge to the south. Even at tidal flux, it is so still and quiet that you can see insects alight on its surface and watch fish take them. Birds in flight can even be identified by their reflection on the river's surface.

Access. The only access necessary (because a craft can easily be paddled up this little river, then back down it) is at a small park in northwest Hoquiam.

Driving Directions. To reach the access park, head north out of Hoquiam on U.S. Highway 101 (Lincoln Street), which turns left (west) near the north edge of town and then swings right at an angle to the northwest just before crossing the Little Hoquiam River. As the highway completes its swing to the northwest, turn left onto Queen

Kayaks on the Little Hoquiam.

Avenue, which becomes Endersen Avenue at the first curve west of U.S. Highway 101. Follow it southwest to a bend in the Little Hoquiam River at a small park and a boat landing. This is the put-in and take-out.

Another way to reach this put-in is to turn left onto Highway 109 after crossing the Hoquiam River on U.S. Highway 101, and head west toward Ocean Shores. In a little more than a mile, turn right onto Spencer Street and follow it over the hill to Lion's City Park. Turn right to skirt the park, then left onto the other end of Endersen Road (Endersen is a road at one end, an avenue at the other).

Description. From the launch site, the river is reflection-still except for the occasional stirring by power boats that also use the boat ramp. Around the first bend upstream, the man-made world is left behind and paddlers enter a kinder, softer realm.

Wonderful woodsy smells take away the exhaust fumes, and bird songs nibble away at the fading echoes of the motors' roar. Hundreds of swallows fill the air at dusk or before a rain, and the only sounds are natural ones as the river weaves its way into the wilderness. Clear-cut scars dominate the landscape, but nature was here first and will endure. Even in the battle-scarred landscape, there are great blue herons, spotted sandpipers, kingfishers, green herons, gulls, nighthawks, robins—and a huge nest of white-faced hornets.

The river loops quietly into the darkening landscape. An insect hatch in the happening: the surface of the river is alive with the multistrikes of tiny fish. Their feeding frenzy makes more noise than passing paddles. A new bridge looms ahead, and the river splits beyond it. The right-hand fork is blocked by fallen trees a few hundred yards in.

The main river meanders and curves for another mile. Then paddlers can head back down the quiet river toward the landing, moving with the tide, watching reflections in the water and nighthawks flit and dive and swoop, gathering insects. It's that kind of river.

Canada geese enjoy riverbank grazing and grooming.

Log storage pilings on the Lower Wishkah River.

33 *WISHKAH RIVER*

Location: Aberdeen, north and northeast
Distance: 7.5 miles
River Time: 2 hours
Maps: Aberdeen (7.5′), Humptulips (15′); NOAA Chart: 18502
Best Season: all year, rainy in winter
Hazards: contrary tides, power boats
Shuttle: 6.2 miles on paved roads
Rating: A, T

Overview. The Wishkah River flows into the Chehalis River in the latter's last mile, virtually at the point where the Chehalis gives up its ghost to Grays Harbor. One of several tidal rivers in the Grays Harbor area, the Wishkah offers exploratory paddle trips on different branches, providing different insights into the area. The Wishkah, which circles through northeastern Aberdeen, flows out of the timbered forestlands from an area that hosts two parts of the Olympic Wildlife Area. It is a slow, narrow river, ideal for beginning paddlers.

Access. The best access to the take-out is from the south side of the Chehalis River opposite the mouth of the Wishkah. The launch site is from a public boat ramp at RM 7.2 on Wishkah Road, which closely parallels the river on the right bank (west of the river).

Driving Directions. To reach the take-out across the Chehalis River from the mouth of the Hoquiam, follow U.S. Highway 101 south from H Street across the bridge over the Chehalis River (highway signs suggest that this is the way to Raymond and West Port). Turn left at the first stop light (the main flow of traffic goes this way) and left again in a few hundred yards onto Boone Street as the road bends to the right, just before the South Aberdeen Fire Station ap-

169

pears on the left. (Since this may be a difficult turn to make in heavy traffic, it may make sense to go beyond the turnoff, double back wherever it is convenient and legal, and, as you head back toward Aberdeen, make the turn to the right.) Boone Street leads to the take-out at the Old West Bridge approach, a public boat access.

To reach the launch site several miles up Wishkah Road, take U.S. Highway 101, going straight ahead on G Street to Market, turning right onto Market to B Street, turning left on B Street and following it north. It forks right to become Wishkah Road. Follow it out of town along the river to the boat ramp only 5 miles from the left turn onto B Street.

Description. The Wishkah River is a small, intimate stream. It seems to have been diked at some time in the past, but whatever human control existed is so far removed in time that it appears natural enough; the banks are well vegetated and the bends seem appropriate. It is mostly a rural river, with a few big trees along its banks and a house or two along the way. A slow-moving fishing boat may come putting along upstream, but there are few power boats in so narrow a river.

The river swings left, then sharply right through marshy lands. It hugs the road between RM 5.4 and RM 5, then swings away into the marsh only to return for another kiss at RM 4.3. At RM 4 it begins a sharp S that ends only as Bear Creek comes in from the left and the river approaches Aberdeen. The last 2 miles of this route flow through an urban area; the final 0.5 mile, through downtown. U.S. Highway 12 crosses the river only a hundred yards from its mouth. The take-out involves paddling across the mouth of the Chehalis as it flows into Grays Harbor.

34 WYNOOCHEE RIVER: Lower Main Stem

Location: north, northwest of Montesano
Distance: 16 miles
River Time: 4 to 5 hours
Maps: Montesano, Wynoochee Valley (15′)
Best Season: all year, due to reservoir release
Hazards: timber trash, sweepers
Shuttle: 15 miles on paved roads
Rating: B–

Overview. The Wynoochee River flows south out of Olympic National Park, but a major dam that makes this river runnable through-

Low water and wide gravel bars on the lower Wynoochee River.

out the year (though it may get a bit lean in late summer and early fall) creates a barrier between the pristine and the merely scenic. Several segments of the upper river are run by kayakers, and canoeists run a 19-mile segment above this lower 16-mile stretch.This segment flows through a broad farming valley to the Chehalis just south of Montesano. It is a pool-and-riffle river with plenty of gravel bars and fine views of low, timbered hills.

Access. The best take-out is at a public fishing area south of Montesano on the Chehalis River, 0.25 mile above the mouth of the Wynoochee. There are two accesses along the Wynoochee Valley Road north of Montesano, one about 4 miles northwest of town at the mouth of Black Creek (RM 5.5), and another at the Old White Bridge Site (RM 16).

Driving Directions. To find the take-out on the Chehalis River a mile south of Montesano, take U.S. Highway 12 to Montesano and turn off onto Highway 107 toward Raymond. Less than a mile south, just past a lumber mill, turn left onto a narrow road that leads to a public fishing access on the right (north) bank of the Chehalis River 0.25 mile above the mouth of the Wynoochee.

To reach any of the accesses on Wynoochee Valley Road, return to

Montesano, head west to Wynoochee Valley Road (which leads toward Wynoochee Dam), and turn right, following it northwest 3 miles to the Black Creek boat ramp left of the road on river left. A run from here to the take-out would be less than 6 miles.

To locate the access at the Cutover Bridge Site, (a shortcut to the Wishkah River) continue north on the Wynoochee Valley Road another 6.2 miles then turn left on the Wishkah–Wynooche Road to an access on the left bank (east side) at RM 13.7. The river is actually accessible from either side of the river at RM 15.7. To reach the right bank (west side of the river) turn west on the Wishkah–Wynoochee Road, which crosses the river on the Cutover Bridge toward Aberdeen. Turn right almost immediately and follow the road 2 miles to the west side of the Old White Bridge Site at the end of the road. To reach the left bank (east side of the river) return to the Wynoochee Valley Road, turn left and drive 2.5 miles to a public fishing access sign and turn left, following the road to the riverbank.

Description. From the Old White Bridge Site the river flows relatively straight for nearly 3 miles, its banks overgrown with grasses, native shrubs, wildflowers and the ubiquitous blackberry. There is an island at RM 14.8, with two small creeks entering the river from opposite sides at the island. The river flows beneath the Cutover Bridge at RM 13.6, bends sharply left at RM 13.2, and begins a series of slow meanders that continue for the next 6 miles.

Leopard frogs frequent Western Washington riparian zones.

Several times the river kisses the parallel roads that embrace it from RM 12 south to RM 2.5, where U.S. Highway 12 crosses the Wynoochee. Throughout this segment the river flows through farmlands, and an occasional barn or farmhouse is visible from the river, but the agricultural scene rarely intrudes upon the river corridor. Wildlife occurs along the river (birdlife, raccoon, deer) and fishermen often ply their sport during their season.

Despite the obvious rural and urban scene of Montesano and the traffic of U.S. Highway 12, which it roughly parallels for a mile or so, the Wynoochee remains relatively wild all the way to its meeting with the Chehalis, south of Montesano. The boat ramp that serves as the take-out for this segment is just a brief paddle to the left (0.25 mile up the Chehalis) from the mouth.

35 SATSOP RIVER: *Lower Main Stem, East and West Forks*

Location: between Aberdeen and Olympia, north of
  U.S. Highway 12
Distance: 10 miles, East Fork; 11 miles, West Fork
River Time: 3 to 4 hours each
Maps: Elma (7.5′), and Wynoochee (15′)
Best Season: all year, except late summer or early fall
Hazards: timber debris, sweepers, pilings in fast water
Shuttle: 11 miles, East Fork; 12 miles, West Fork on paved roads
Rating: B

Overview. The lower Satsop and its lower East and West forks constitute a network of small, intimate clear-water streams that flow out of the southern Olympics through rain-forest vegetation. The area is largely cut over, but the second growth areas still offer high-quality habitat for paddlers. One of the launch sites is in a state park, another in one of Weyerhaeuser's premier parks. The pool-and-drop character of the river offers challenges to the paddler, and the scenery provides an exciting and varied backdrop.

Access. The two uppermost accesses, one on each fork, lie in parks, one of which offers a steep but manageable launch. The two suggested take-outs, both on paved roads, have boat ramps, one off U.S. Highway 12 near the town of Satsop (within sight of the defunct nuclear power plant cooling towers).

174

Schafer State Park launch site, East Fork, Satsop.

Driving Directions. To reach the take-out boat ramp, travel eastward on U.S. Highway 12 between Montesano and Elma near Satsop (the boat ramp is accessible only from the east-bound lane but there are several traffic cross-overs near the bridge). A shuttle vehicle can be left here if paddlers plan to paddle the main stem river from the forks, a 4-mile run. An alternate take-out lies on the Chehalis River 0.25 mile above the mouth of the Satsop. Take Keyes Road south off U.S. Highway 12 just east of the bridge and follow it 1.3 miles to a public fishing access with a boat ramp.

The boat ramp on the lower West Fork lies less than a hundred yards above the forks and can readily be used as a take-out for runs on either fork or as a launch site for the short run to U.S. Highway 12.

To reach this handy access, head east from the boat ramp on U.S. Highway 12 to the next exit (Satsop) and turn left (north) toward

175

Satsop. Then turn left again into that small town and head west to Brady, another tiny town. In Brady turn right onto West Satsop Road and drive about 3.5 miles to the boat ramp, a public fishing access right of the road, on the right bank of the West Fork.

To reach either of the two put-in points from this access, return to West Satsop Road and turn right, heading north again on West Satsop Road. To reach the West Fork put-in, stay left at the fork in the road in 0.25 mile and follow this narrow winding road to Weyerhaeuser Timber Company's Swinging Bridge Park (the last 0.5 mile is through a tunnel of trees). Launch on the right bank at RM 7.2 of the West Fork for a 7-mile run to the forks access or an 11-mile run to U.S. Highway 12.

To reach the East Fork put-in, turn right from the forks access and head north on West Satsop Road. At the fork in the road 0.25 mile north of the forks access, turn right and follow the signs 4.7 miles to Schafer State Park. It is possible to launch from the park with a short carry to the river. (The park can also be reached by taking the East Satsop Road north from the Satsop-Brady road just west of Satsop, east of the bridge across the Satsop.)

Description. The East Fork in popular Schafer State Park is lean in late summer, but most of the year it is readily runnable by canoe or kayak. It will be challenging at times because of the tight corners, timber debris and sweepers, but it offers an insight into an isolated, intimate, rain-forest river.

Almost immediately paddlers will float beneath the bridge that brought them to the park. As the river bends out of sight of the bridge, a tiny creek enters on the right, followed by Decker Creek also on the right (RM 12). The river corridor is lined with tall trees, and even though roads parallel the river on opposite sides, they rarely intrude upon the river itself.

Below Decker Creek the river makes a jog to the right, then a quick jog to the left over a rocky bed, to meet the Middle Fork, which enters from the right at RM 11. A long gradual curve to the left and the mouth of Cook Creek appears, at RM 10. At this point East Satsop Road is near enough to touch as the river curves back to the right for a straight mile.

A trio of tiny creeks enter from the right between RM 9.2 and 8.2 as the river meanders through its flood plain for the final 2 miles to a confluence with the West Fork at RM 6.4. The 4-mile run from here to the U.S. Highway 12 take-out will be described after the description of the West Fork run.

The West Fork put-in at RM 7.2 is marked by a footbridge across the river, the namesake of Swinging Bridge Park. Almost immediately there is a sharp turn to the right, and the park is lost from sight in a narrow gorge overhung with huge rain-forest trees. The road is very

Small raft on the Satsop.

near the river for the next 5 miles but so far above it that it never really intrudes.

Three small streams enter from the left in the next 3 miles. The gorge and forest end, and meadows appear. Deer may be seen, as well as raccoons and muskrats, even foxes and numerous species of birds, especially in late spring and early summer. At RM 3.7 the river makes a sharp bend to the right, then at RM 3, an even sharper bend back to the left. The final 3 miles of the West Fork meander through meadowlands, as the river takes on a pool-and-drop character, flows beneath the Middle Satsop Road (thc onc that leads to Schafer Park), and enters a small gorge in its last 0.5 mile to join with the East Fork in a huge deep pool.

From the forks down, the river slows, meanders more widely through its floodplain, creates a few islands and flows through farmlands. At RM 3 it straightens for a run through some old bridge pilings just above the Satsop-Brady bridge, then a railroad bridge and the double span of the U.S. Highway 12 bridge. The take-out is on the left bank immediately below the highway bridge.

36 CHEHALIS RIVER: *Porter to Montesano*

Location: between Olympia and Aberdeen
Distance: 20 miles
River Time: 5 to 6 hours
Maps: Montesano, Malone (15')
Best Season: all year
Hazards: sweepers, logjams, high water
Shuttle: 18 miles, all paved road
Rating: B

Overview. This long, looping stretch of the Chehalis offers excellent paddling on a clear-water river with numerous gravel bars from which to fish or on which to picnic or even camp (though for the most part it flows through private property; be sure to camp below mean high water level or obtain permission from the local landowner). An easy river flowing through a broad valley, this segment provides good fishing as well as occasional views of distant mountains and nearer, forested (and clear-cut) hillsides. Several of its tributaries are also canoeable.

Access. The best access lies at the put-in near Porter and at the take-out south of Montesano, but additional access is possible at at least

The Chehalis River and bridge (not an access) south of Elma.

two points in the lower 7 miles of this run at the mouth of the Satsop (RM 20.5) and at RM 17.3 off Brady Loop Road—if anyone has cleared the trail from the road to the river (it was not cleared the summer of 1988).

Driving Directions. From U.S. Highway 12 at Montesano, take the Highway 107 road south toward Raymond. Less than a mile south of town, immediately after passing a lumber mill on the left, turn left to a public fishing access on the right bank of the river, 0.25 mile above the mouth of the Wynoochee River. Leave a shuttle vehicle here.

Return to U.S. Highway 12 and head east toward Elma, then southeast toward Porter. Turn right (south) at the northwest edge of Porter, toward Rony and South Bank Road, crossing the railroad tracks and the Chehalis River. As the bridge grade drops, turn left into the parking area for a public fishing access. The launch site (boat ramp) is on the southwest bank of the river beneath the bridge at RM 33.2 (Note: this is also the take-out for Trip #37.)

To reach the access at the mouth of the Satsop, turn off U.S. Highway 12 at the Satsop Exit (north to Satsop, south to the access) onto Keys Road. Access lies less than 2 miles from U.S. Highway 12.

Red osier dogwood is a common riverside plant in Western Washington.

To reach the Brady Loop Road access, turn off at the Brady Exit about 2 miles west of the Satsop Exit, head south (Brady is north) on Henry Foster Road, which turns right to become Valentine (all part of the Brady Loop Road). Public fishing access exists—if the trail has been cleared—near a farmhouse south of the loop road.

Description. The Chehalis River is a slow, lazy river in this stretch with a few easy drops. From the launch site on the left bank, the river flows northwest for almost 2 miles, gradually leaving the highway and flowing through farmlands. A short distance below RM 32 it starts a big S curve left, then right, approaching the left edge of its floodplain. It curves less sharply for another big S bend—right, left, right—as Eaton Creek enters on the left (RM 28.6) and Mox-Chehalis Creek enters on the right (RM 27.8).

The river straightens for more than a mile, paralleled by the South Bank Road and the railroad. Delezene Creek enters from the left

(RM 26.8). At RM 26—just after a powerline crossing—a third big S bend begins just south of Elma. Although the river is crossed by a bridge carrying the South Elma-Workman Road at RM 23.8, there is no access.

The river flows almost due west as it passes beneath this bridge, curving in gradual bends for the next 3 miles. Workman Creek enters from the left at RM 22.7, Fuller Creek from the left at an island at RM 21.4, and Newman Creek from the right at RM 20.8. Just after the river flows beneath the bridge carrying Keys Road across the Chehalis, the Satsop River comes in from the right. The access here is between the Satsop mouth and the bridge.

The river has been gaining volume, has gradually become a bigger, broader river. From the mouth of the Satsop, the Chehalis again flows along the south edge of the valley, paralleling the railroad for more than 2 miles before making a sharp right turn into a broad area, from which Moon Slough loops around an island in the vicinity of RM 17. The access off Brady Loop is onto the right bank of Moon Slough.

Elizabeth Creek enters from the left, opposite the island (RM 17); and Stevens Creek, from the left on a sharp bend at RM 15.8, where the river touches the railroad embankment. Another mile of relatively straight river and Metcalf Slough enters from the right (RM 14.7). This area is tidal, and at extremly high tides the impact can be felt. One more big sweeping bend, right, then left, and the river parallels Highway 107 south of Montesano, makes a final sharp right and flows beneath a pair of bridges. Take out at the boat ramp on the right before reaching the bridge.

37 *CHEHALIS RIVER/ LOWER BLACK RIVER: Oakville to Porter*

Location: southwest of Olympia, near Oakville
Distance: 9.2 miles; from Black River, 18 miles
River Time: 3 hours; from Black River, 6 hours
Map: Malone (15′)
Best Season: all year, spring through fall
Hazards: sweepers, logjams
Shuttle: 8 miles, paved road
Rating: B–/A+

Overview. The Oakville-to-Porter run is a pleasant paddle on a moderate-sized river that flows through a broad agricultural valley, rural rather than developed. The banks are well vegetated with shrubs, grasses, second-growth timber, and non-timber species. The lower Black River is shallow and narrow with a gravel bottom and abundant aquatic vegetation; its lower 2 miles revert to southern swamp—slow with heavily wooded banks. The Chehalis between the mouth of the Black River and the Oakville access flows through farmlands with fields often nudging the river itself. It has plenty of gravel bars and lots of timber trash as well.

Access. All three accesses are easy to find; two are just off U.S. Highway 12, and one is only a mile by paved road from this main highway. The take-out is just northwest of Porter; the launch site is just northwest of Oakville. The launch site on the Black River (take-out for Trip #38) is at the U.S. Highway 12 bridge crossing, west of Rochester and east of Oakville.

Driving Directions. To reach the take-out for this segment, which is the launch site for Trip #36, turn west from U.S. Highway 12, just northwest of Porter, cross the river and turn left into a public fishing access parking area. Leave a shuttle vehicle here, return to the highway and turn right, heading southeast toward Oakville.

To reach the put-in 0.25 mile northwest of Oakville: either (1) go to the outskirts of Oakville and turn right near Oakville High School onto the Elma-Gate Road, which doubles back along the northwest between the highway and the river. The put-in is an undeveloped public fishing access on a slough that communicates with the Chehalis (at low water it may be blocked by a beaver dam). The access is left of the road traveling northwest from Oakville.

Or (2) heading southeast from Porter to Oakville on U.S. Highway 12, turn left 3 miles southeast of Porter onto Blockhouse Smith Road just after crossing Gibson Creek. This road is also the Elma-Gate Road and will save a couple of miles and provide an opportunity to see the river, which it parallels for a mile or so.

To reach the Black River access off U.S. Highway 12 (for the longer trip on the lower Black and a longer stretch of the Chehalis) drive through Oakville, heading eastward toward Rochester; but about 2 miles east of Oakville, immediately after crossing the Black River, turn right into a small parking area by a boat ramp on the left bank of the river.

Description. At the launch on the Black River, masses of aquatic vegetation almost obstruct a paddle route down its narrow course through this section. Some route-finding may be necessary at the low water levels of late-summer. The river flows past farm houses and barns, past pastures and clearings. After a couple miles of extreme meandering over a shallow gravel bottom with occasional riffles, the river slows to sluggish, winding between steep, thickly wooded banks.

From the mouth of the Black at RM 47, the Chehalis flows through a broad, intensively farmed valley where some fields extend right to the river's edge. It meanders widely, involving a sloughlike backwater on the right 0.25 mile below the confluence, and another on the left 1.5 miles below the confluence. At RM 45 the river reaches the left (southwest) aspect of its flood plain to parallel the railroad and Garrard Road for a mile, then flows beneath the bridge (RM 44), which carries the South Elma-South Bank Road into Oakville.

From the bridge, the river curves toward the northeastern edge of its flood plain through a heavily wooded area on the outskirts of Oakville. At RM 42.2 the undeveloped access, which may be difficult to see from the river unless it's been scouted carefully beforehand, lies on the right bank of a slough (it may be a beaver pond at low water levels).

Water lilies bloom in many backwater sloughs.

CHEHALIS
RIVER
(Oakville to Porter)

For the next mile, the river hugs the northeastern side of its floodplain, except for a loop to the left, then makes a sharp turn back toward Blockhouse Road. It then swings slowly to the west, running along the southwestern edge of the floodplain for a mile (RM 40 to RM 39) not far from Cedarville Road. Then it loops back to the middle of the valley to flow northwestward for several miles through alternating open areas and forested stretches, with pastureland and farms on either side.

Rock Creek enters from the left at RM 39.2 just as the river bends east. Cedar Creek enters from the right at RM 38.7, and Gibson Creek enters from the right at RM 37.2. The broad valley is full of isolated ox-bow lakes and gravel deposits left by an earlier river. At RM 36 the river again hugs the northeastern edge of its floodplain briefly, paralleling the Burlington Northern Railroad tracks for 0.25 mile before it begins a major double loop just south of Porter to again nudge the railroad for 0.25 mile at RM 34. It loops left around Porter, and the take-out lies on the left bank (across the river from Porter), upstream from the bridge.

38 BLACK RIVER

Location: southwest of Olympia, near Rochester
Distance: 12 miles
River Time: 5 to 6 hours
Maps: Rochester, Oakville (7.5'), Rochester (15'); DNR Map:
  "Capitol Forest"
Best Season: all year
Hazards: vegetation masses, fallen trees, sweepers
Shuttle: 10 miles on paved roads, ideal for bicycle
Rating: A

Overview. The Black River southwest of Olympia is unique, a southern river placed in the Pacific Northwest, a placid fairyland stream, full of beautiful butterflies and birdlife during the summer months, fantastic colors in autumn, and wildflowers in spring and summer. Even in winter this black-water river suggests *The Hobbit* or *Willow* in its scenic beauty. Curling around the southeastern base of the Black Hills below Capitol Forest, it has excellent access, yet remains one of the most remote rivers in the state. Even in this 12-mile segment it offers great variety.

Access. There is public access on Highway 121 south of Littlerock, at the oxbow bend of the river off Moon Road west of Rochester, and on U.S. Highway 12 between Rochester and Oakville. There is also

BLACK
RIVER

Author Verne Huser poling a deep, quiet stretch of the Black River.

access to the Chehalis River 1.5 miles northwest of Oakville, about 5 miles below the mouth of the Black River for anyone who wants to make a longer run.

Driving Directions. To reach the take-out on U.S. Highway 12 about 3 miles east of Oakville (4 miles west of Rochester), take Exit 88 off of I-5 south of Olympia and head west toward Aberdeen and "Ocean Beaches" on U.S. Highway 12. The boat ramp lies on the left bank, south of the highway before it crosses the Black River bridge— immediately downstream from the bridge at RM 4.2.

To reach the modest boat ramp off Moon Road, return to U.S. Highway 12 and head east 2 miles to Moon Road, which T's in from the left. Turn left onto Moon Road, then right in 0.25 mile onto School Land Road and head east toward Rochester for 0.25 mile. The access is to the left of the road on the left bank of the river at RM 8.7.

To reach the access on Highway 121 south of Littlerock, continue east on School Land Road into Rochester, then turn left onto Highway 121 and head north toward Littlerock for about 5 miles. The put-in for this trip is at a public fishing access left (west) of the highway, about 2 miles south of Littlerock, at RM 16.2.

(To reach the alternate access on the Chehalis River northwest of Oakville, return to U.S. Highway 12 and head west. Just west of Oakville, turn left onto the Blockhouse-Smith Road that follows the river more closely than does U.S. Highway 12; within a mile there is an access point left of the road on the right bank of the river. See map #37.)

Description. Protected by marshes and pasturelands, both public and private, the Black River barely flows for the first 5 miles of this 12-mile segment. It is a long, deep lake fringed by water lilies, often overhung by streamside vegetation. Carved by the massive glacial melt in the Cascades at the end of the last ice age, the Black River takes its name from its dark water, strained with the tannin of its decaying vegetation, and from the Black Hills, its source.

The first 3 miles hug the east side of the valley, never more than 0.5 mile from the highway and the adjacent railroad. (They are hidden by dense vegetation that screens all but the sound of an occasional logging truck.) At RM 13 there is a private boat ramp on the left bank without an access road; crayfish sun themselves on the corrugated concrete.

From this point the river swings gradually toward the west side of the valley. Mima Creek enters from the right at RM 12.3, 0.5 mile before the river nudges the Burlington Northern Railroad (RM 11.8) near the Black River Wildlife Area. From that point it heads southwest for 1.5 miles, past isolated homes and tall conifers, one on the right sporting an active osprey nest.

The river skirts a couple of farms near the northwest edge of Rochester and changes character completely at RM 10. It begins to loop in sharp, sudden curves, its bottom shallows into a series of dips, and the current picks up. The bottom is covered with thick mats of aquatic vegetation, and in some places the clumps actually interfere with navigation, forming obstacles that nearly block the river.

Passing beneath a spur railroad bridge at RM 9.3, the river goes into its oxbow between RM 9 and RM 8. The access at RM 8.7 is so subtle that paddlers may miss it unless they are looking carefully. The river is less than a dozen yards wide here. At RM 7 it passes beneath Moon Road between U.S. Highway 12 and Gate, which lies only a few hundred yards from the river.

The river continues its looping course, hemmed in by dense vegetation. Its bottom is shallow, full of aquatic growth in places but scoured clear in others. The current increases from time to time (thus the scouring effect). Rafts of water crowfoot, forget-me-nots and wild mint grow in the water during the summer. Ancient pilings and dead logs host lush gardens of grasses, wildflowers and shrubs.

When the U.S. Highway 12 bridge comes into view, it is time to take out—unless paddlers plan to continue downstream another 4 miles to the Chehalis (the lower Black embraces the Chehalis Indian Reservation, and paddlers may encounter fish nets), and 5 more miles on the Chehalis River to the access northwest of Oakville. This is farming country with some fields extended to the water's edge. There are small drops and deep pools, a few trashy corners with sweepers and snags, but lots of gravel bars.

An osprey nest sits in a tall conifer along the Black River.

Hanging gardens over conglomerate bluffs, West Fork, Humptulips River.

39 *HUMPTULIPS RIVER:* West Fork

Location: north of Hoquiam/Aberdeen, southwestern Olympic
   Peninsula near Humptulips Store
Distance: 6.5 miles
River Time: 1 to 2 hours
Map: Quinault Lake (15′)
Best Season: all year, but best at high water, November to May
Hazards: logjams, sweepers
Shuttle: 4.5 miles on paved roads, mountain bike ideal
Rating: B

Overview. A rain-forest river rising along the southern boundary of Olympic National Park, the Humptulips River is charming for its name as well as its lush vegetation and pristine character—even in an area where the forests have been butchered for decades. This short segment of the West Fork flows past steep bluffs of conglomerate and sandstone, alternating between pools and shallows with occasional modest drops. There are logjams and sweepers, sometimes a tree across the river, but such obstacles can be portaged. There is disagreement over the meaning of Humptulips—either "cold area" or "tough to pole."

Access. Access to the take-out is off Donkey Creek Road east of U.S. Highway 101, north of the Humptulips crossing. The launch site is off Fish Trap Road, a logging road branching off Donkey Creek Road a few miles north.

Driving Directions. To reach the take-out, turn right off U.S. Highway 101 onto Donkey Creek Road about 3.5 miles north of where 101 crosses the Humptulips River near the village of Humptulips. Drive 4.9 miles to a bridge across the West Fork of the Humptulips; just beyond the bridge turn left onto a dirt road that gives access to the river. Leave a shuttle vehicle here; a mountain bike is ideal for the short shuttle.

To reach the launch site, return to Donkey Creek Road and turn left. Drive 2.9 miles to Fish Trap Road (unmarked), and turn left again. Follow this road to a river access in about two miles to put in on the left bank of the river (RM 43.2).

Description. The West Fork of the Humptulips flows south from the launch site (RM 43.2) over a shallow, gravelly bottom, through lush rain-forest vegetation (big-leaf maples festooned with ferns overhanging the river, hemlocks and western red cedar). It pools occasionally, swinging back and forth between gravel bars and dropping over minor rapids. After a few hundred yards it bends right, then sharply left to serpentine southward for a mile to the mouth of Rainbow Creek entering from the left (RM 41.2). Fish Trap Road crosses Rainbow Creek by a bridge adjacent to the river, and the river turns abruptly right, then right again in two sharp bends to form three sides of a square box between dense streamside vegetation.

The river then loops north for a final bend through Olympic National Forest and flows southwest. The hidden bluffs begin to emerge to form vertical river banks of conglomerate. Tiny falls and dripping springs water the ferns and flowers that grow on the bluffs, a spectacular sight. Newberry Creek enters from the right (RM 40). The river loops its way south, then east in two big horseshoe bends, and approaches Donkey Creek Road.

Donkey Creek enters from the left (RM 38.4), and the river bends southward again. It nudges the road (RM 38), unnoticeable because it is well above the river and screened by vegetation, before swinging

HUMPTULIPS
RIVER
(West Fork)

END

37

38

Donkey Creek Road

DONKEY CREEK

39

40

NEWBERRY CREEK

RIVER

41

Olympic

National

Forest

RAINBOW CREEK

Fish Trap Road

42

HUMPTULIPS

START

43

Miles

0   1

back to the west for 0.25 mile to the mouth of a tiny tributary creek (RM 37.7) at which the river swings south again for its last meandering mile to the take-out. The bluffs have been left behind, and on the flats the river swings between gravel bars and overhung banks where a tree occasionally falls to block the entire river or create a sweeper.

The take-out lies at a wide gravel beach on the left bank as the river swings east to flow beneath the Donkey Creek Road bridge (RM 36.7).

From this point it is possible to continue downstream all the way to Grays Harbor. Many of the river access points in the next several miles (not shown on map) have been closed off by local landowners in protest to a county ban on gravel mining (intended to protect water quality and enhance the river's ability to propagate anadromous fish). There is rough access beneath the U.S. Highway 101 bridge, on the north bank of the river (RM 23.1), and a good public access less than a mile downstream, off a spur road from 101 marked "Public Fishing Access" that turns west about a mile south of the Humptulips Store.

Sun and shadow and shallow water on the Humptulips typify late-summer paddling in the southern Olympic Peninsula.

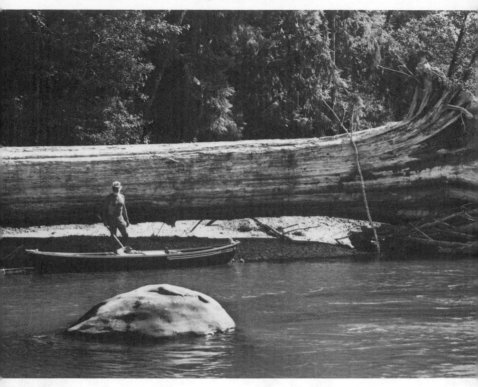

Large trees dominate the Queets River shoreline.

40 *QUEETS RIVER: Sam's Rapid to Hartzell Creek*

Location: southwestern Olympic National Park
Distance: 12 miles
River Time: 3 to 4 hours
Map: Salmon River (15')
Best Season: all year, but best at high water, November to May
Hazards: Class II rapids, sweepers, logjams
Shuttle: 12 miles by gravel road, mountain bike
Rating: C+ (the most difficult in this book)

Overview. The Queets is a big, fast, cold river flowing out of the Olympic Mountains through coastal rain forest. Its frequent winter floods rearrange the logjams and create new sweepers. Its serious

Class II rapids challenge paddlers, but it is the best wildlife river in the Northwest with elk, deer, otter, beaver, mink, coyotes, osprey and eagles as well as an occasional bear. Its meandering floodplain offers spectacular views of the Olympic peaks, its ultimate source, and its waters are milky with rock flour from its headwater glaciers.

Access. All of its launch sites and take-out points, with a single exception, are reached from the Queets River Road in Olympic National Park, which leaves U.S. Highway 101 in the northern part of the Quinault Indian Reservation. The single exception is an access at the confluence of the Clearwater and Queets rivers on the Quinault Indian Reservation.

Driving Directions. To reach the Queets River Road, turn north off U.S. Highway 101 about 7 miles east of the bridge across the Queets River, near its mouth (17 miles west of Quinault Lake), and follow it north, then east. The suggested take-out at Hartzell Creek (RM 11) is only 2 miles from the highway. Turn left and leave a shuttle vehicle here (a mountain bike will serve).

To reach any of the alternate accesses or the proposed put-in, continue eastward on the gravel road toward the Queets Campground at the end of the road. At the campground, scout out the river: launch can be made above or below Sam's Rapid (RM 23.2), which lies on the bend of the river that wraps around the campground.

Alternate access points lie at Streater Crossing (RM 17.1) about halfway between Sam's Rapid and the proposed take-out, and at River View (RM 14.4) about 3 miles southwest of Streater Crossing (4 miles northeast of Hartzell Creek).

To reach the access beneath the bridge across the Queets at the confluence of the Clearwater and the Queets, go back to U.S. Highway 101 and turn right (west) for about 2.5 miles, and turn right onto the Clearwater Road. (See Map #41.) Technically, permission to use this access requires permission from the Quinault Indian Tribe.

Description. From Sam's Rapid, a long curving rock garden on the bend of the river at the campground put-in, the Queets flows southwest through a broad valley. Ancient trees that have survived the clear-cutting so devastating in this area appear along the bank: gigantic old Sitka spruce, huge cottonwoods, big-leaf maples covered with mosses, and massive Douglas fir.

The river meanders through braided channels from one side of its floodplain to the other; first hugging the north side (RM 22.3), then bending south past the Queets Ranger Station to approach the south side (RM 21.3), then heading west for a mile, splitting around small, low islands throughout these first few miles. Beware of logjams and sweepers, large rocks and confluence currents.

Queets River, with the Olympic Mountains in the background.

The Queets flows around a sizeable island just above RM 20. Either side is normally passable, but paddlers must judge the flow for themselves in low water because annual winter floods rearrange the bars and islands (and logjams), determining where the current goes. The river bends southwest briefly, then northwest even more briefly, then southwest once more before starting a sharp horseshoe bend left, then back to the right. At the end of the horseshoe turns, the river is again hugging the ridge on the right (north) at RM 18.

The straight stretch from RM 18 to RM 17 flows southwest through excellent elk habitat. A favorite spot for elk is the meadowland near the mouth of Phelan Creek, which enters the Queets from the left (south) at RM 17.8. Streater Crossing (RM 17.1) on the right (south) bank is a logical half-way point roughly 2 hours (6 river miles) from Sam's Rapid. To find this spot from the river, scout it out from the access road on the drive up and establish a marker that will identify it from the river when it is reached.

Below Streater Crossing the river makes an abrupt left turn, with a nasty little rock and sweeper on the far left. At low water it may be difficult to avoid, but it can be lined on the right. Several small rapids (rock gardens) interrupt the flow of the Queets in this vicinity; they require some skill in maneuvering to negotiate successfully. The road roughly parallels the river from RM 16.8 to the take-out; but it is rarely visible, never obtrusive. Mount Olympus is visible to the east from several points along this stretch of river.

Matheny Creek flows into the Queets from the left (RM 15.8) just before the river enters a shallow S bend that ends at River View, a possible access (RM 14.4) on the left bank. The river corridor is well vegetated throughout this stretch, though massive clear cuts can be seen on the surrounding hillsides outside the gerrymandered national park boundaries. Tacoma Creek enters from the right (RM 13.1) and the road, always on the left bank, parallels the river closely for the final 2 miles.

The toughest rapid on this stretch of river lies immediately below Tacoma Creek's mouth. (No doubt the rocks that make the rapid were brought down the tributary stream during a heavy rain.) There is a ledge system of bedrock on the left from which to scout the lower part of this long rapid. Below the rapid the river continues in a southwestern direction, with a steep bank on the left and open meadows on the right where elk may be seen. A small rapid (more of a rock garden) leads to a deep pool at a slight right bend of the river just above the take-out (from the rocky left bank Mount Olympus is visible).

41 CLEARWATER RIVER

Location: southwestern Olympic National Park
Distance: 11.5 miles
River Time: 3 to 4 hours
Map: Destruction Island (15')
Best Season: all year, but best at high water, November to May
Hazards: sweepers, logjams, moderate rapids
Shuttle: 8 miles on paved road
Rating: B–

Overview. True to its name, and despite massive clear-cut logging in the drainage, the Clearwater is as healthy a stream as paddlers can canoe in western Washington. It abounds in aquatic invertebrates that provide good fish food. It is an intimate river, small and winding in its upper reaches; broader but nonetheless charming in its lower miles. Although logging operations scar the surrounding hills, little evidence

Sweepers and gravel bars along the Clearwater at low water.

of timber cutting exists on the river itself. Its shoreline vegetation is dense and natural, excellent wildlife habitat.

Access. Access to the Clearwater is by way of the Clearwater Road, a paved second-grade highway (narrow with plenty of turns) which heads north from U.S. Highway 101, a few miles east of the 101 bridge over the Queets, a few miles west of the Queets Road.

Driving Directions. To reach the Clearwater, turn north off U.S. Highway 101 about 2.5 miles west of the Queets Road (see Trip #40), about 4.5 miles east of the 101 bridge over the Queets (19.5 miles west of Lake Quinault). In about two miles the road crosses the Queets River on a new (1988) bridge near the mouth of the Clearwater. In less than a mile beyond the bridge—just after a DNR logging road turns right—turn left into the DNR Clearwater Picnic Bar on the left bank of the river 0.8 mile from its mouth.

To reach the put-in, return to the Clearwater Road and turn left (north), following it 8 miles to where it crosses the Clearwater River on a high bridge (stay left at all branch roads). The put-in is immediately beneath the bridge, but it is a steep, rough carry down the north side of the road, west of the river.

Description. At low water levels, the first 100 yards of this run requires the paddlers to lie flat in the bottom of the canoe to avoid overhanging trees. No doubt at higher water levels there is more current in midriver, away from the sweepers. In short, the first few hundred yards suggest the intimate character of this clear-water river: lots of shallows, riffles, sweepers and minor logjams that can be gingerly negotiated.

At the put-in bridge (RM 12.3) there are deep, deep pools that serve as reflection ponds for everything in sight. But the huge pools narrow and shallow to barely negotiable chutes and to riffles so shallow it may be necessary to walk the craft through in late summer. The river flows due west after it breaks out of its initial bend at Rocky Rapid (so-named on the USGS maps, but not all that severe). Then it makes a short, sharp horseshoe (Skookumchuck Rapid lies at the apex of the horseshoe but is no big deal), bends right into a sweeping curve that ends flowing westward again just as Shale Creek enters from the left (RM 11). All this area is engulfed in dense rain-forest vegetation.

Mink Creek enters from the right (RM 10) on a mile-long nearly straight stretch flowing southwest. Wide gravel bars force the current against the bank and into the trees in many places. A named rapid—Barker—lies halfway between the mouth of Elkhorn Creek and Cougar Creek, which enters on the right. The Clearwater bends northwest, then southeast in a sharp horseshoe; Cougar Creek enters at the apex of the bend (RM 8.8). The bend opens toward the south for half a mile, and Parsons Rapid, another insignificant riffle, shows up on the map at RM 8.

Then the river makes a quick right and left in rapid succession, as Hunt Creek enters from the left (RM 7.8) to mark another westward run for half a mile. As the river swings south again there is Preachers Rapid (RM 7.1)—why did the mapmaker name all these insignificant rapids? None of them are worthy of the name. Below Preachers Rapid, the last named rapid on the river, there is a half-circle loop to the west with the river flowing southeast for nearly a mile after it breaks out of the bend (RM 6 to RM 5.2) and heads for the access road.

Wildcat Creek enters from the left (RM 5.3) just before the river bends sharply south, continuing to the southwest as the river hugs the left side of its floodplain, with the road just above. Another horseshoe bend to the west and back subtracts a mile as the river reaches for its

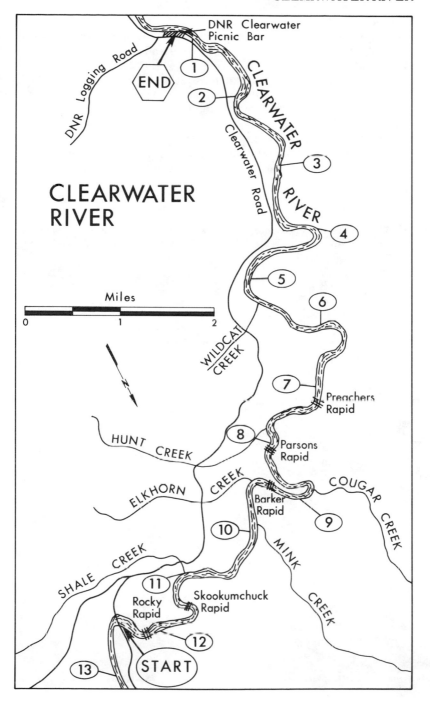

DNR Clearwater
Picnic Bar

CLEARWATER RIVER

END

CLEARWATER
RIVER

DNR Logging Road

Clearwater Road

Miles

0   1   2

WILDCAT CREEK

Preachers
Rapid

HUNT CREEK

Parsons
Rapid

ELKHORN CREEK

Barker
Rapid

COUGAR CREEK

MINK CREEK

SHALE CREEK

Rocky
Rapid

Skookumchuck
Rapid

START

confluence with the Queets and once more edges the road (RM 3.7). The river valley has widened during the past few miles, and in its final three, it flows through a broad valley where a few farms suggest civilization but where logging is still king.

Informal, private and pirate campsites appear along the last 2 or 3 miles of the Clearwater, but a broad gravel bar on the left, opposite a low cut bank on the right, marks the take-out at a DNR picnic area that is used all summer for family camping. Paddlers will see the new Queets bridge if they go too far, but the road is so near the last 0.75 mile that they could take out along the road (it is a bit steep) or at the boat ramp beneath the new Queets bridge at the confluence.

A ground cover of ferns and sorrel along the Clearwater.

Backpackers along the Hoh River near its mouth.

42 HOH RIVER: Oxbow to DNR Cottonwood Camp

Location: west of Olympic National Park, south of Forks
Distance: 5 miles; 14 miles with permission
River Time: 1 hour; 2 hours with permission
Maps: Forks, Destruction Island (15')
Best Season: all year, but best at high water, November to May
Hazards: logjams, sweepers, fast, cold water
Shuttle: 4.5 miles on gravel and paved roads, mountain bike ideal
Rating: B+

Overview. The Hoh is the famous rain-forest river that serves as the centerpiece of the developed portion of Olympic National Park, but the segment described here lies below the park. A big, cold, fast river even in its lower portions, the Hoh offers excellent fishing and challenging boating, though this segment has no real rapids. It flows between parallel roads—U.S. Highway 101 on the south side and the Lower Hoh Road to Oil City on the north side—but meanders and braids its way through a mile-wide floodplain to offer picturesque vistas and interesting wildlife habitat.

Access. Access is from two Department of Natural Resources (DNR) facilities: a boat ramp just off U.S. Highway 101 near its Hoh River crossing and a campground off the Lower Hoh Road. It can be run all the way to its mouth if permission can be obtained from either the private property owner on the north bank of RM 1 or the Hoh Indian Tribe on the south bank near the river's mouth.

Driving Directions. To reach the take-out for this short, fast trip, turn off U.S. Highway 101 about 15 miles south of Forks onto the Oil City Road (Lower Hoh Road) that roughly parallels the river on its north side. About 2.5 miles down that road, turn left toward DNR's Cottonwood Recreation Area, a primitive camping area that also serves as a boat launch. The shuttle is so short that a mountain bike makes an ideal shuttle vehicle.

To reach the launch site, return to the Oil City Road and turn right (east) toward U.S. Highway 101. Turn right onto U.S. Highway 101 and go about a third of a mile to a spur road turning off to the left (east) into a DNR campground and fishing access area. Simply follow the signs to the boat launch area. Don't cross the bridge; the turnoff is north of the bridge over the Hoh.

Rain-forest vegetation of Olympic Peninsula rivers.

Description. The Hoh is deep, swift and cold at the launch site (RM 15.3), which is heavily used by fishermen with power boats. It's a busy place for a paddle craft, but within a quarter mile the river takes the craft beyond the bend, beneath the bridge and west for a mile. RV's may be camped on the left bank as the river bends south. Paddlers may want to stop at RM 14 and visit the largest known spruce tree, the Helen Clapp Spruce. It stands, without its top, less than a quarter mile from the river. It was once 248 feet high, but it lost its top in a storm; it is 17 feet 9 inches in diameter and was once calculated to contain 50,500 board feet of lumber.

As the river continues its course south, it flows over a riffle (mild rapid) just as it touches the roadbed of U.S. Highway 101 (RM 13.6). Below the riffle it begins a westward curve, flows around an island (RM 13.4), passes a favorite fishing hole known as Allen's Bar (RM 13) and swings north. The river braids and meanders through massive gravel bars, swinging back and forth between the boundaries of its floodplain. At RM 12, where it reaches the northern edge of the floodplain in one of its curves, is a DNR fishing access with limited parking, accessible from the Oil City Road. The river swings in a big bend around a promontory gravel bank that serves as Cottonwood Campground (DNR) at RM 10.7, the take-out.

If permission has been obtained to take out at the mouth of the river, another 8 miles downstream (not on accompanying map), paddlers will see the river broaden slightly and continue its meandering, braided course to tidewater, then fluctuate with the tide in its lower few miles. It splits around a few sizeable islands, forms a few sloughs at high tide, and offers an interesting paddle that few people experience.

43 QUILLAYUTE RIVER/ LOWER DICKEY RIVER

Location: west of Forks, Olympic Peninsula
Distance: 5.7 miles/5 miles
River Time: between 1 and 2 hours each
Map: La Push (15')
Best Season: all year, but best at high water, November to May
Hazards: sweepers, logjams, contrary tides
Shuttle: 4 miles on paved road
Rating: A, T

Overview. The Quillayute, one of the shortest rivers in Washington at less than 6 miles, is totally tidal—as is the section of its tributary, the Dickey River, covered here. True rain-forest rivers, they both provide delightful paddling through corridors of gigantic trees covered with mosses and ferns. There are logjams, to be sure, and sweepers, but the flow is so mild in these relatively flat-terrain rivers that they present no real problem unless the whole river is blocked (as has been true on the lower Dickey in recent years).

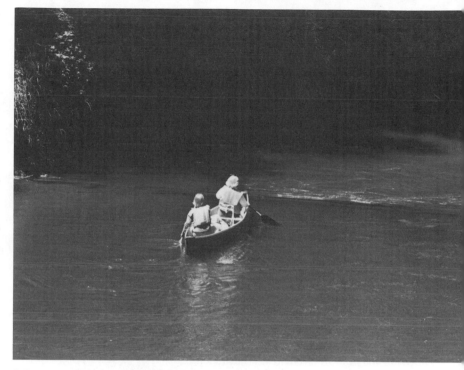

Submerged logs create hazards in the Quillayute River.

Access. Both the put-in and the take-out for the Quillayute are from boat ramps directly accessible from La Push (Mora-Ocean Beach) Road, west of Forks, off U.S. Highway 101. The Dickey is accessible from Minnie Smith Road, but such access may be meaningless if the recent massive logjam still exists on the lower Dickey. The best access to the Dickey, which involves traveling upstream, is from the boat ramp on the Dickey a mile west of the ranger station in this portion of Olympic National Park. This is also the lower access suggested above for the Quillayute.

Driving Directions. To reach the Quillayute (and the put-in for an upstream exploration of the Dickey), drive west from the La Push turnoff from U.S. Highway 101 about a mile northwest of Forks. Follow this road all the way into Olympic National Park, about 14 miles from U.S. Highway 101.

Heading west, note Leyendecker County Park. Its boat ramp will serve as a launch site for the trip down the Quillayute, which begins at the confluence of the Soleduck and the Bogachiel rivers (this is also the take-out for Trip #44).

The Quillayute begins at the confluence of the Bogachiel (left) and the Soleduck (right) and flows westward to the Pacific.

A mile past (west of) the park entrance station, turn left to a boat ramp on the left bank of the lower 0.1 mile of the Dickey. This boat ramp will serve as a take-out for a 4-mile trip down the Quillayute from its point of origin or a put-in for a paddle (or pole) up the Dickey River. Spot a shuttle vehicle here; a bicycle is ideal for this short shuttle.

To reach the launch site at Leyendecker County Park, retrace the route 4 miles to the boat ramp between the rocky Soleduck and the Bogachiel.

Description. The Bogachiel drops over a ledge into one of the deepest pools on a Northwest river; this is where the Quillayute is born. From the confluence of the Soleduck and the Bogachiel (RM 5.7), the Quillayute narrows briefly as it flows out of this deep pool. The road to its mouth crosses the Soleduck on the right as the Quillayute makes a long, straight, slow run toward the Pacific between borders of tall trees. There are massive gravel bars along the river.

At RM 4.3 the river begins a big bend to the south, forming a U open to the north; it is almost an oxbow that takes more than a mile of river to make less than half a mile of westward progress. Much of the land enclosed by the loop is open and developed, but there are always massive trees in view, relics of earlier times or second- and third-growth evidence that this is great tree-growing country.

Shortly after the river heads west again (RM 3.3) it enters Olympic National Park and flows slightly north of west for nearly 2 miles, making its final left turn to the ocean just below the mouth of the Dickey, which enters from the right (RM 1.6). The take-out lies on the lower Dickey only 0.1 mile from the Dickey's entry into the Quillayute. Simply paddle upstream on the Dickey, which enters from the right, and the boat ramp is on the right (river left).

The Dickey is a smaller, more intimate river. Its navigability varies from season to season as logjams come and go. Paddling or poling up the Dickey from the Quillayute offers a special experience as the river meanders through lush rain-forest vegetation.

Boat ramp at River Mile 6.6 on the Bogachiel.

44 BOGACHIEL RIVER:
Bogachiel State Park
to Confluence

Location: south and west of Forks, western Olympic Peninsula
Distance: 15.4 miles
River Time: 4 to 5 hours
Maps: La Push, Forks (15')
Best Season: all year, but best at higher water, November to May
Hazards: logjams, sweepers, modest rapids
Shuttle: 14 miles
Rating: B

Overview. The Bogachiel River, which means "muddy waters," is a
frequently flooding river of the Olympic Peninsula, one that has occa-

sionally washed out U.S. Highway 101. It is also a prime steelhead stream and receives much fishing pressure. Most of its course flows through private lands, but there are a few public access points. Much of it is forested, though there is also agricultural land along the way, largely unobtrusive. Its waters clear whenever the rains stop long enough to let the river drop its suspended load of rock debris.

Access. Access to the put-in is provided at Bogachiel State Park on U.S. Highway 101, a few miles south of Forks. Access to either of two suggested take-out points is from La Push (Mora-Ocean Beach) Road, which turns off of U.S. Highway 101 a mile north of Forks.

Driving Directions. The ultimate take-out for this segment of the Bogachiel is its end—its confluence with the Soleduck to create the Quillayute. To reach this point, drive north from Forks on U.S. Highway 101 and turn left (west) onto the La Push Road (it becomes the Mora or Ocean Beaches Road as you stay right at the Y). Drive 7 miles to Leyendecker County Park (only 0.3 mile from the Y), where a boat ramp lies between the Bogachiel, which flows from the left, and the Soleduck, which flows from the right.

An alternate access (a possible put-in for a shorter run downstream or a take-out for a shorter run from the state park) lies off La Push/Mora Road about 3.4 miles west of Leyendecker County Park. Return to Mora Road and turn right (east); it joins the La Push Road at the Y. Continue another 3 miles eastward and turn right to a public fishing access about a mile south.

To reach the launch site at Bogachiel State Park, return to Mora-La Push Road and turn right (east) and return to U.S. Highway 101; turn right, go through Forks and south to the state park on the right (about 7 miles after returning to U.S. Highway 101). Turn into the state park and seek a logical launch site, perhaps near the picnic shelter at the upper end of the park, near the Bogachiel Bridge.

Description. From the park launch area (RM 15.6) the Bogachiel flows west for half a mile, turns gradually south, then abruptly northwest (RM 14.7) through DNR lands, and then heads northward in a series of loops, one of which kisses U.S. Highway 101 (RM 12.8). The river is clear most of the year and flanked by gravel bars backed by tall trees; the banks are well wooded.

Grader Creek enters from the right (RM 10.4) shortly after the river turns west and leaves U.S. Highway 101 for the last time. Mill Creek enters from the right (RM 9.7) as the river continues to flow slightly north of west. At RM 8.7 a state steelhead pond lies just off the river on the right bank, accessible by way of Bogachiel Way southwest of Forks. In another few hundred yards the Calawah River joins the Bogachiel from the right (RM 8.4).

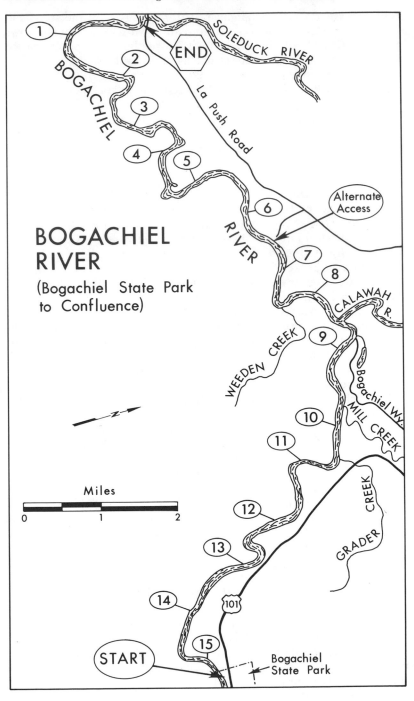

Moving southwest now, the river turns gradually south (RM 8). Weeden Creek enters from the left, and the river makes an abrupt bend to the northwest, then back to the southwest, and the alternate access appears as a boat ramp on the right.

Below this intermediate access point the river continues to bend back and forth, making a southward swing for a mile, then turning abruptly west at a big pool (RM 4.6) on the bend. A slough comes in from the right just beyond the bend (RM 4.4). In half a mile the river heads north again, then begins a broad double U (W?) as it continues its meandering course to its confluence with the Soleduck. The final mile it flows almost due north.

45 *WILLAPA RIVER: Lower Main Stem and Forks*

Location: south of Aberdeen; South Bend, Raymond and east
Distance: 10 miles plus sloughs
River Time: 3 to 4 hours
Maps: Raymond (15'), South Bend (7.5'); NOAA Chart: 18405
Best Season: all year
Hazards: contrary tides, power boats
Shuttle: 10 miles, paved road
Rating: A, T

Overview. The lower Willapa River and its convoluting sloughs offer an interesting look at a small West Coast timber and fishing town as well as an opportunity to paddle some quiet rural waters and explore a protected saltwater bay. The fishing is good in the Willapa at certain seasons, and the boating is dependable year-round because of the tidal influence on this entire segment. Oyster fishing still thrives in the bay, but timber is king in Raymond, a town bisected by the river.

Access. Excellent access exists off U.S. Highway 101 northwest of South Bend, about 2 miles from the river's mouth as it flows into Willapa Bay. An excellent access lies at the mouth of Wilson Creek at RM 12, a 10-mile shuttle for a 10-mile run.

Driving Directions. To reach the take-out, drive west out of Raymond through South Bend. At the northwest edge of South Bend to the right of the highway is a small turnout with a boat ramp on the left bank of the lower Willapa River as it broadens to become Willapa Bay. Leave a shuttle vehicle here.

To reach the put-in, return to Raymond on U.S. Highway 101 and cross the bridge over the Willapa River. Almost immediately beyond the bridge, turn right onto the Willapa-Monohan Landing Road and follow it about 4 miles to the public fishing access to the right of the road at the mouth of Wilson Creek. There is a boat ramp here on the right bank of the river and ample parking.

Description. The Willapa River is placid at the launch site, unless the wind is up. The river, tidal all the way, hugs the road for the first 0.5 mile, past tall scattered conifers and ancient pilings. It bends left to flow west and run straight for about a mile through low-lying marshlands, then bends left again to head southwest. At RM 10.4 a major slough branches off to the left (south) to double back to a point very near a loop of the river a mile above the launch site.

The river broadens and becomes almost sluggish unless the tide is flowing out. Two other minor sloughs branch off to the right in this vicinity and another branches off to the left just as the river reaches

Mouth of Wilson Creek, launch site for Willapa River.

the east edge of Raymond, a town totally dominated by the timber industry.

From here for the next 3 miles the river loops through town, faced with timber-related activities including a massive Weyerhaeuser sawmill. The small homes of a typical company town dot the slopes beyond the timber-processing facilities and huge piles of sawdust awaiting export. Sizeable ships enter the harbor to carry away what used to be a waste product but is now a valuable resource.

The South Fork of the Willapa meets the main stem near the west edge of town and can be explored as a side trip. From the junction of the two forks, the river flows southwest, broad and busy with boating traffic (commercial fishermen, oyster gatherers, timber-related vessels). It's an interesting experience to dodge the power crafts in a paddle-powered boat, but most of the power-boat pilots are courteous drivers.

Another small slough heads south as the river narrows at RM 5, and South Bend begins on the left bank. The Willapa swings past South Bend in a broad U as a slough that branches off to the right at RM 2 sends its tentacles almost to the base of the open end of the U. The boat ramp that serves as take-out is hard to miss; it lies just beyond the last buildings at the western edge of South Bend.

46 GRAYS RIVER/ SEAL SLOUGH

Location: northeast of Astoria; OR; northeast of Grays Bay,
*   Columbia River; south of Aberdeen/Hoquiam*
Distance: up to 10 miles, Grays River; 2 miles on Seal Slough;
*   7 more miles on nearby Deep River*
River Time: 3 miles per hour, slack tide
Map: Grays River, WA/OR (7.5'); NOAA Charts: 18521, 18523
Best Season: all year, but best in rainy season September
*   through May*
Hazards: contrary tides, wind on the Bay
Shuttle: 3 to 10 miles, but no shuttle necessary
Rating: T, A below covered bridge, B above it

Overview. Grays River is a small tributary of the Columbia River named for Captain Robert Gray, who discovered the Columbia (the river was named for his ship). Seal Slough is a tributary of Grays River that enters it about 2 miles from its mouth. Nearby Deep River feeds into Grays Bay about 2 miles west of the mouth of Grays River. All these segments are tidal. Washington's only extant covered bridge lies

Covered bridge over Grays River.

on Grays River at RM 9.6, a mile above the upper extent of tidal influence. While this region is rainy, it offers excellent birding and unique paddling opportunities through a historical landscape.

Access. The only real public access is available at a boat ramp less than 0.5 mile south of the Rosburg Store near the Rosburg Community Hall, but there are informal launch sites at a private campground less than a mile from the mouth of Deep River; at a private boat dock at Devils Elbow, the last bend of Grays River before it enters the Bay; at a gravel bar at RM 8; and another near the confluence of the East and West forks of Grays River north of Highway 4. There is a public fishing access stile at the covered bridge that might also be used for launching a canoe under the covered bridge.

Driving Directions. The best launch site may also be the best take-out if the tides are played right—the boat ramp one third of a mile south of Rosburg at RM 4.2. To reach it, turn south off Highway 4 at the Rosburg Store between Naselle and Cathlamet onto Highway 403 (Altoona Road; the sign says "Dead End—7 miles"). Turn right onto a parallel road west of the highway heading south just as the highway rises to cross Grays River on an elevated bridge. The unmarked road leads to the Rosburg Community Hall. The boat ramp is a few dozen yards southwest of the building.

To paddle downstream to the Bay, and perhaps explore Seal Slough on the way, paddlers may want to leave a shuttle vehicle (a bicycle is

ideal) at Devils Elbow (RM 1), about 3 miles by road from the launch site. To reach it, return to Highway 403 and turn right, cross the bridge and head south for less than 3 miles to Mattson Road and turn right. Park alongside the road, preferably on the left-hand (southwest) side. It is best to ask permission to use the private dock to the right of the road for launching or taking out.

To reach two other accesses, return to Highway 4 and turn right, heading northeast. Take Covered Bridge Road south off Highway 4 at the village of Grays River, and follow the road to the covered bridge. On the south side of the river are the public access stiles that offer rough access. The gravel-bar access at RM 8 (above the covered bridge) can be reached by following Covered Bridge Road upstream after crossing the bridge to a point about 2 miles above the bridge, where a rough road offers access to a big gravel bar left of the road, on the left bank of the river.

For a longer run of Grays River above tidewater, launch at the rough access near the confluence of the river's main forks. Return to Highway 4 and head east toward Cathlamet. Two miles from Grays River village the highway crosses Grays River. Turn left onto Sauterland Road, and follow it to where it peters out at a school bus turnaround, then follow the track to the river bank (RM 11.4) (a standard vehicle will make it in most road conditions).

To reach the launch site on Deep River, return to Highway 4 and head west. Just after crossing Deep River, turn left onto Oneida Road. There is rough access from the road 4.7 miles from the highway and a commercial campground access 5.2 miles from the highway (the paving ends 3.7 miles from Highway 4).

Description. From the boat ramp near the Rosburg Community Hall, paddlers can head upstream toward the covered bridge—if the tide is coming in—or downstream on the outgoing tide. Either route offers a unique experience.

Heading upstream between blackberry-festooned banks, paddlers weave northeast through agricultural lands about 3 miles to the Village of Grays River. (A new boat ramp is scheduled to be located here at a tiny park at the south edge of town.) From the village the river swings abruptly south and then east through pasturelands, to flow beneath the covered bridge (RM 9.6). Going upstream beyond this point is likely to be difficult for two reasons: (1) the tidal influence subsides a mile below the bridge, and (2) in summer the water can become shallow.

Heading downstream, paddlers also encounter the blackberry banks and thick bank vegetation of red osier dogwood and viburnum as the river loops widely through dairy farms and pasturelands, bordered by dark, brooding Sitka spruce trees that in places overhang the shore. It turns left to flow south for a mile, then swings right to flow westward, past occasional rural homes and backyard logging operations where second- and third-growth forests survive and wildflowers (lotus, jewelweed, tall orchids) abound in summer.

Just below RM 2 Seal Slough enters from the right and can be followed all the way to the old Finnish Church just off Highway 4, a full 2 miles north by water. Taking a right turn at the fork 1.3 miles upstream, the paddler can go almost another mile up the branch of the slough that leads to Kandoll Road a few hundred yards west of Rosburg.

The lower 2 miles of Grays River are totally tidal, lined with tall trees and houses, boat docks and moored boats. If the tide is right, boaters can paddle down to the Bay, explore its northern reaches, even enter Deep River 2 miles to the west. If a shuttle vehicle has been left at the lower end of Deep River, paddlers can take out there along a stretch of river, again lined by small houses, fishing shacks and moored boats.

To run the upper stretch of Grays River, launch at the forks access (RM 11.4) off Sauterland Road. From here the river is small, winding and shallow in summer, with splits around brushy gravel islands and tight corners, a moderate B river unless it is flooding (which may be much of the year, given the heavy rains of the area). The river flows south as it begins a sharp S curve which ends beneath the Highway 4 bridge. Then it moderates as it enters agricultural lands, still lined by trees and shrubbery as it meanders through the valley to flow beneath the covered bridge.

47 COWLITZ RIVER:
Massey Bar to I-5 Bridge

Location: near Toledo
Distance: 7 miles
River Time: about 1.5 hours
Map: Castle Rock (15′)
Best Season: all year, fine in summer, fall
Hazards: minor rapids, sweepers, logjams
Shuttle: 8 miles
Rating: B–

Overview. The Cowlitz, one of the premier steelhead fishing rivers of the Northwest, is a big, deep, lovely river where it flows beneath and alongside I-5, north of Longview and Kelso. It is more of a mountain stream, a big one to be sure, but a mountain stream nonetheless,

Paddling the Cowlitz in a wood-and-canvas canoe.

east of I-5 in the vicinity of Toledo. This river offers views of both Mount Rainier and Mount St. Helens, excellent fishing, birding and boating on a big open river that moves with good speed. It is rural but with little evidence of the adjacent farms, except for the launch site in a cow pasture.

Access. The take-out, a public fishing access, lies just downstream from the I-5 bridges crossing the Cowlitz. It is reached from a local access road southwest of Toledo. The best launch site, another public fishing access, lies off a local access road northeast of Toledo.

Driving Directions. Although the take-out is almost immediately beneath the I-5 bridge over the Cowlitz, it is complicated to reach: take Exit 60 off I-5 and head east toward Toledo. After 2 miles turn right at the Jackson Highway (Highway 505) in Toledo, and follow it through town, crossing the Cowlitz and turning right from Highway 505 onto South Jackson Highway 0.3 mile from the bridge. Follow this highway southwest to Mandy Road, turn right, then left onto River Road, and follow it under the I-5 bridges to the public fishing access just west of the freeway.

To reach the launch site, return to Toledo and head north out of town on Winlock-Toledo Road, veer right at the north end of town and follow signs toward Lewis and Clark State Park (North Jackson Highway). At the Cowlitz Mission Historic Site, turn right, then left in 0.3 mile onto Spencer Road, then right onto Buckley Road, which leads to what looks like a dead end. Turn right onto a gravel road that winds down a hill into a cow pasture. On an open flat by the river, the launch site is on the right bank of the river—a boat ramp heavily used by steelhead fishermen using drift boats or dories.

Description. From the launch site the river is broad and fast, clear and shallow, its banks rip-rapped with basalt blocks. In low water there is a riffle just below the put-in. The river flows through open country with a fringe of vegetation along the banks, swinging gradually to the left to pass Toledo, which lies on the right bank in about 3 miles. Bill Creek enters from the right just before Toledo.

The river passes beneath the Highway 505 bridge and swings right, still broad and shallow for the most part, though a few deep stretches alternate with riffles. Walking access used by fishermen in steelhead season lies along the inside (right bank) curve at the bend below town. The river gradually deepens, flows around an island or two, and swings left at a point where the river is less than a mile from I-5 and the sound of highway traffic may intrude.

The river parallels I-5 about a mile from the freeway as it flows south, then curves right to flow westward in a long, straight stretch for more than a mile. The take-out lies on the left bank 100 yards below

225

the double span of the I-5 bridges. There are a few good river access points along River Road, which is the extension southwest of the road along the Cowlitz.

48 COWLITZ RIVER: Trout Hatchery to Massey Bar

Location: northeast of Toledo, southeast of Chehalis
Distance: 7 miles
River Time: 1.25 hours
Maps: Castle Rock and Toutle (15')
Best Season: all year, especially summer, fall
Hazards: minor rapids, sweepers, logjams
Shuttle: 7 miles
Rating: B

Overview. One boater has called this stretch "the best river this side of the mountains for new boaters." That's a personal opinion, but it does suggest the quality of experience available on the upper Cowlitz. Mount Rainier can be seen from the put-in and from several points along the river. And there is plenty of wildlife to see—bald eagles and osprey, deer and beaver. The river is broad, tree-lined and rural, almost wild in nature, its forested banks giving it a more pristine appearance that its surroundings suggest.

Access. Both the take-out at a public fishing access and the launch site at the State Trout Hatchery are reached from Spencer Road, which roughly parallels the river on its north side. The shuttle drive offers views of both Mount St. Helens and Mount Rainier.

Driving Directions. To reach this segment take Exit 60 off I-5 and head east to the town of Toledo. Turn left (north) in 2.5 miles onto the Winlock-Toledo Road. Pass Toledo High School and, in less than a mile, veer right at the Y toward Lewis and Clark State Park. At the Cowlitz Mission Historical Site 1.3 miles from the Y, turn right (south), then left after only a third of a mile onto Spencer Road heading east.

At Buckley Road, less than a mile from the Mission, turn right and follow it to the end of the pavement; turn right on the gravel road toward the public fishing access that has a boat ramp and ample parking. Leave a shuttle vehicle here. This is also the launch site for Trip #47.

Return to Spencer Road and turn right (east). In 4.8 miles turn right into the State Trout Hatchery; 0.7 mile from the turnoff is a boat ramp at the far (downstream) end of the public fishing access area and considerable parking. Many people camp here as well.

Description. From the double boat ramp at the western end of the public fishing access area at the State Trout Hatchery, the river is broad and shallow, its banks well forested. The river bends to the left (there is private access on the left bank, just below the bend), and there may be ospreys and eagles, kingfishers, and great blue herons fishing the clear waters in this vicinity.

As the river bends to the right again, it becomes braided, but the main channel is obvious. Pasturelands lie on the left, a slight bluff on the right. There are many islands for lunch stops and excellent birding in summer. Skook Creek enters on the right a mile before the river gathers itself together, still broad, clear and fast. It makes one more swing to the north against the bluffs before it reaches the take-out boat ramp on the right bank of a shallow bend to the south.

The Cowlitz River, with Mount Rainier in the background.

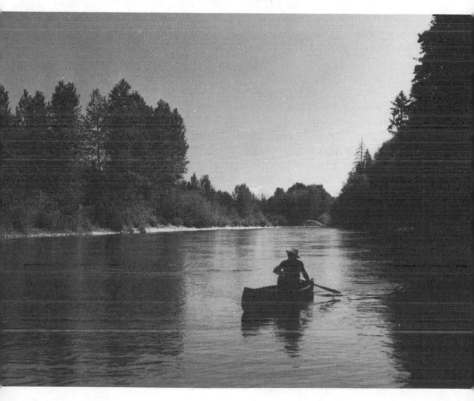

49 COWLITZ RIVER: Salmon Hatchery to Trout Hatchery

Location: *northeast of Toledo, southeast of Chehalis*
Distance: *8 miles*
River Time: *1.5 hours*
Maps: *Toutle and Onalaska (15')*
Best Season: *all year, best in summer*
Hazards: *Class II rapids, sweepers, logjams*
Shuttle: *7 miles*
Rating: *B+*

Overview. This uppermost segment of the Cowlitz, just below Mayfield Dam, gets heavy fishing use, but it is a more challenging stretch of river for paddlers (in fact, the Cowlitz gets progressively more challenging with each segment, moving upstream). This is the most scenic and pristine of the Cowlitz segments as well, a mountain stream that yields salmon and steelhead as well as trout. Its rapids are easy, except for one, and that one can be lined or portaged on the right (though it is not that difficult a rapid).

Access. Both the take-out (the put-in for trip #48) and the launch site are reached from Spencer Road, which parallels the river on the north side. The whole Cowlitz complex lies just a few miles south of U.S. Highway 12.

Driving Directions. To reach this segment take Exit 60 off I-5 and head east to Toledo, turning left as Highway 505 T's into the main north-south street in Toledo, which becomes the Winlock-Toledo Road. In less than a mile, just past Toledo High School, veer right at the Y toward Lewis and Clark State Park, and head northeast on Jackson Highway. At 1.3 miles from the Y, turn right at the Cowlitz Mission Historic Site, left after a third of a mile onto Spencer Road, and head east toward the Cowlitz Trout Hatchery and the Cowlitz Salmon Hatchery.

After following Spencer Road for 5.3 miles, turn right at the sign to the Cowlitz Trout Hatchery, and follow the road to the public fishing access, a double boat ramp 0.7 mile from the turnoff. Leave a shuttle vehicle here. This is also the launch site for Trip #48.

To reach the launch site, return to Spencer Road and turn right (east). There is a stop sign after about 5 miles at Fuller Road. Go straight ahead 0.2 mile to a yield sign which offers a free right turn; stay right (essentially straight ahead) into the Cowlitz Salmon Hatch-

The upper Cowlitz run offers some lively water.

ery, and follow the road to the public fishing access several hundred yards below the barrier dam below Mayfield Dam. The launch site is on the right bank of the river.

Description. Immediately below the boat ramp the river bends sharply to the left. Within a quarter mile you are out of sight of civilization, heading south along a pristine corridor between tall trees where migrant eagles and ospreys fish, along with the resident kingfishers and great blue herons. The river is shallow except at flood stage (and its level is controlled to some extent by the upstream dams) and amazingly intimate for so large a river.

The river bends sharply to the right 1.5 miles below the launch site, as two small streams enter from the left and an island appears in midriver. Either side of the island will normally be negotiable, and in low water the flow will be obvious. From this bend, the river flows northwest for another 1.5 miles between tall cottonwoods and conifers with an understory of alders and numerous native shrubs.

The river bends sharply once more to the left near Spencer Road, and a small creek enters from the right after it flows beneath the adjacent road, creating one of the most serious rapids on the run, a modest Class II (it can be scouted from the road while driving to the launch site). The river flows south briefly, then bends back to the west as a steep bluff on the left bank gives the river relief.

Once the river takes its westward course, it flows relatively straight for 3 miles, the last 0.5 mile along the Cowlitz Trout Hatchery grounds. The take-out lies at the lower (downstream) end of the hatchery property.

Note: The three Cowlitz segments (Trips #47–49) can easily be run in a day. The entire 22-mile stretch from the salmon hatchery to the I-5 take-out has been poled in 4 hours and 15 minutes of river time in midsummer when it was relatively low. Any one of the stretches can easily be done after work on a late-spring day when daylight hours are long, and all three can easily be done on any weekend of the year.

50 LOWER KALAMA RIVER

Location: 40 miles north of Portland
Distance: 8 to 10 miles
River Time: 2 to 3 hours
Map: Kalama (7.5′); NOAA Chart: 18524
Best Season: all year; may be too low in late summer, too high
in winter (flood stage)
Hazards: sweepers, logjams, modest rapids
Shuttle: 6.4 miles on paved roads (take-out unpaved)
Rating: B+

Overview. One of the best steelhead tributaries of the Columbia, the Kalama has some fine whitewater stretches above this segment. At the lower reaches, this clear, swift stream provides a few challenging miles of modest rapids before it breaks out of its confining canyon a few miles from the Columbia, into which it flows. The paddler is suddenly thrust into a modern world of freeways, nuclear power plants, and grain elevators feeding ships carrying food for a hungry world. Despite logging trucks on adjacent roads, rural homes and vacation cabins along its shoreline, the Kalama is a pleasant run less than an hour from Portland.

Access. One take-out on the lower 0.5 mile of the river and another on the right bank of the Columbia River only a few dozen yards downstream from the Kalama mouth offer excellent access at the end of this trip. Since Kalama River Road hugs the river much of the distance of this segment, there are a number of possible launch sites right from the road.

Driving Directions. The take-out for this segment can be reached from I-5 by taking Exit 32 (Kalama River Road) 2 miles north of

Kalama (or 7 miles south of the Highway 4 exit [Exit 39] south of Kelso). Head west over the railroad tracks to a public fishing access left of the road, on the last bend of the river.

To reach the access on the Columbia River itself, follow the county road past the public fishing access to where it officially ends. Then turn left, following signs that lead to a Sportsman's Club, but instead of turning into the Sportsman's Club (left), go straight to the Columbia River beach on the right bank, a few dozen yards below the mouth of the Kalama.

To get to the launch areas, return to the county road which crosses over the railroad tracks and I-5 to become Kalama River Road, and follow it east (upstream). There are several roadside accesses, but the farthest upstream that is still safe Class II water is opposite a red barn on the left, 6 miles from the I-5 exit. The rough launch site is right (south) of the road, on the right bank of the river.

Other possible launch sites include the one at Prichard's Western Angler 0.6 mile downstream from the red barn put-in (RM 8.6); public fishing access areas at RM 6 and RM 5.4, and on the left bank just above Modrow Road Bridge (RM 3.5). Modrow Road crosses the Kalama River at this point as it heads south, then east to access the residents living south of the river.

Description. At the red barn put-in there is only roadside parking, and there is no boat ramp, just a rough carry to the right river bank. The river gets busy quickly. An island forces a choice of routes—right is usually better. A big rock in midriver offers another challenge, then Prichard's Store appears on the right bank across the road.

Below Prichard's Store is a solid Class II rapid that can be cheated, but its tailwaves offer some nice haystacks (standing waves). Kingfishers and ouzels make their presence known. Beaver cuts line the bank, and peeled sticks cover the sandy bottom in the eddies. Fern-festooned cliffs steer the river through the forested gorge, and a kinky cable crosses the river not far above the Fawlett Bridge, where a Class II swing rapid lies on a sharp left-hand bend.

This rapid can be tricky. The current flows strongly along the left bank, which is essentially a cliff, and the right side of the river is a rock garden. Strong eddies mark the confluence of counter currents, but experienced paddlers should have few problems here (if this rapid, which can be scouted from the road, seems too challenging, launch just downstream at the public fishing access a mile below).

A waterfall on the left adds to the scenery as does the presence of birds (Steller's jays, chickadees, more kingfishers). The river widens to shallow riffles, and a series of waterfalls appears on the left as houses appear on the right along with some domestic mallards. The public fishing access lies on the right, well used by steelhead fishermen, and a large rock splits the river (the right channel is normally the way to go).

Licorice fern growns here in the shade of Douglas fir, western red cedar, hemlock, grand fir, maple and alder. Old houses appear on the left bank, and the river glides past a fish hatchery near a problem rapid. A gravel bar on the right pinches the river into a narrow turbulent channel on the left—watch for logjams and sweepers. Another access lies at a riffle on a big bend where cabins appear on the left, and there is a pipeline on the right at a green bridge with a logjam.

The green gas pipeline and a gauging station mark the entry into

The Trojan nuclear power plant, across the Columbia from the mouth of the Kalama.

civilization. A trio of yurts appears along the river, and soon the Modrow Bridge comes into view with the fishing access on the left bank under the bridge. The river is out of the canyon now, and it widens and slows. Oak trees appear and planted orchards. Red osier dogwood lines the banks and tall cottonwoods replace the conifers of the canyon.

There are a few sweepers, but the current is now so slow that they seem not to matter. The Trojan Nuclear Power Plant appears to the west—it lies just opposite the mouth of the river—and gulls join the ravens and robins that now occupy the shoreline. Livestock appears, and the sound of the freeway intrudes even as more beaver cuttings suggest wilder times and places. The final mile is almost sluggish, and on windy days you will probably want to take out at the public fishing access 0.5 mile above the mouth rather than fight the wind and experience the waves on the Columbia.

FURTHER READING

No book will turn a novice into a proficient paddler, but there are a number of books well worth reading to whet the appetite for the sport, to aid in understanding some of the basic concepts, and to gain the feel of river travel. Reading about river running will provide prospective paddlers with the background to lead them in appropriate and safe directions.

Both *Canoe* (P.O. Box 3146, Kirkland, WA 98083) and *Paddler* (4061 Oceanside Blvd., Suite M, Oceanside, CA 92056) magazines offer good technique articles, how-to and where-to pieces, and just plain fun, interesting and educational articles. They also review books that offer insights into the literature of the sport.

How-to Books

One of the best basic books on both canoeing and kayaking is the ACA's (American Canoe Association) Instructors Manual: *Canoeing and Kayaking* by Laurie Gullion. Bill Mason's *Path of the Paddle* is a classic book on canoeing that belongs in every paddler's library. The new revised edition of *Sports Illustrated Canoeing* by David Harrison and the American Red Cross *Canoeing* are both good basic books.

The Complete Wilderness Paddler by James Davidson and John Rugge offers good practical lessons for paddlers. The authors plan and execute a major expedition. For those interested in saltwater paddling there are Derek C. Hutchinson's *Guide to Sea Kayaking* and John Dowd's *Sea Kayaking.*

William Nealy's *Kayak: An Animated Guide to Intermediate and Advanced Kayak Technique* and *Whitewater Kayaking* in the Adventure Sport Series may seem a bit advanced for beginning and flatwater paddlers, but they offer good technique.

Where-to Books

At least five books about Washington rivers have appeared during the past decade. Some of them include lakes and saltwater segments; most of them deal largely in whitewater. There are river segments in this book that duplicate a few found in these other books, but those segments are simply good, popular runs and belong in any book that pretends to be representative.

Werner Furrer's *Water Trails of Washington* (1979) is the earliest of these. *Paddle Washington* by Dave LeRoux and Martha Rudersdorf (1984) covers five or six rivers in each of several parts of the state.

Gary Korb's *A Paddler's Guide to the Olympia Peninsula,* a comprehensive treatment of 40 Olympic Peninsula rivers, deals largely in whitewater (20 of the 40 river segments are Class III or above, and four more are Class II+ segments).

Both of Douglass North's books—*Washington Whitewater 1* and *2* —concern whitewater, though some of the runs described are relatively modest ones. Phil Jones's *Canoe Routes: Northwest Oregon* includes five trips in Washington, four river segments and one saltwater paddle. All three of these books are published by The Mountaineers.

General Background

River Reflections, a collection of river writings that this author edited in 1984 and that was reissued as a paperback in 1988, contains excerpts from 43 writers who dealt with rivers in some way. The anthology includes excerpts from Roderick Haig-Brown, whose *A River Never Sleeps* includes descriptions of fishing trips on several rivers covered in this book.

For outdoor humor it is difficult to beat Patrick McManus' *They Shoot Canoes, Don't They* and his other books about hunting and fishing, camping and boating. McManus lives in eastern Washington.

Natural History Books

Any of the field guides in the Peterson series are good to have along on a river trip, those that help you identify birds, mammals, amphibians and reptiles, trees, wildflowers, butterflies, animal tracks, even rocks and minerals. A good reference to bird and animal tracks is The Mountaineers' *Animal Tracks of the Pacific Northwest.* The Mountaineers' *Northwest Trees* and a Nature Study Guide, *Pacific Coast Tree Finder,* will help identify the numerous trees and some of the shrubs found along the rivers.

Birds of North America by Robbins, Bruun, Zim and Singer is particularly good.

River Protection Books

Tim Palmer's *Endangered Rivers* is the best book dealing with the history of river conservation. American Rivers, Inc. has produced a number of documents that may be useful to river conservationists.

The Mountaineers' *Washington's Wild Rivers: The Unfinished Work,* by Tim McNulty with photographs by Pat O'Hara, includes a list of Washington State rivers deserving protective legislation.

INDEX

VERNE HUSER has been a professional river guide for over 30 years. Called "the dean of river writers," he has authored four books on river recreation and has contributed to many magazines, including *Audubon, Backpacker, Sierra, Sports Illustrated,* and *Canoe.* Huser has also worked as a National Park Service ranger and naturalist, a public relations director, and free-lance photographer. A longtime Washington State resident, he now teaches in New Mexico and spends half the year in Washington.

Other books for paddlers from The Mountaineers:

KAYAKING PUGET SOUND, THE SAN JUANS & GULF ISLANDS:
45 Trips on the Northwest's Inland Waters
Randel Washburne. Route information for area from Canada's Gulf Islands
to the shores of Tacoma, plus the unique Hood Canal. $12.95

DISCOVER SOUTHEAST ALASKA WITH PACK & PADDLE, 2nd Ed.
Margaret H. Piggott. The paddle trip included in this hiking/paddling guide-
book is a 12-day journey from Juneau to Angoon. The route includes
Admiralty Island and some of Alaska's best wildlife-sighting areas. $12.95

WASHINGTON'S WILD RIVERS: *The Unfinished Work*
Tim McNulty; photos by Pat O'Hara. Graceful prose and spectacular, full-
color photos combine in this large-format, hardcover book to create a trib-
ute to Washington's wild and free-flowing rivers. $14.98

CANOE ROUTES: NORTHWEST OREGON
Philip Jones. Details, maps and photos for 50 one-day flatwater trips in
Lower Columbia River and Willamette Valley, and the north ocean coast.
$12.95

PADDLING HAWAII
Audrey Sutherland. A paddler's guide to exploring the secluded coves,
jungle streams and wild coasts of the Hawaiian Islands. $12.95

WASHINGTON WHITEWATER: The 34 Best Whitewater Rivers
Doug North. Full information on put-ins, take-outs, river characteristics,
mile-by-mile river logs & maps, for all skill levels. $16.95

BOATER'S SAFETY HANDBOOK
Quick help for boater and boat emergencies: safety equipment, distress
signalling, fire, sinking, bodily injuries, illnesses. $3.50

AFOOT & AFLOAT SERIES
Marge & Ted Mueller. Outdoor recreation guides for hikers, boaters, bicy-
clists, to Puget Sound's fascinating shoreline. $12.95 each volume.
—Middle Puget Sound & Hood Canal
—The San Juan Islands, 2nd Ed.
—North Puget Sound
—South Puget Sound

SOGGY SNEAKERS, 3rd Ed.
Willamette Kayak and Canoe Club. Guide to more than 200 river, stream,
and coastal runs in Oregon, for kayakers, canoeists, and rafters. $18.95

Ask for these at your local book or outdoor store, or phone order toll-free
at 1-800-553-4453 with VISA/Mastercard. Mail order by sending check or
money order (add $2.00 per order for handling and shipping at book rate,
plus $1.00 additional per book for UPS/First Class if desired) to:

The Mountaineers Books
1011 S.W. Klickitat Way, Seattle, WA 98134

Ask for free catalog